Contents

Preface

In this new title to the SEB series, Chris Vidler provides a very clear, accessible and stimulating analysis of operations management. Chris is an experienced teacher, examiner and trainer who has extensive knowledge and experience of the business world. In this book, he draws on that knowledge and experience to include a wide range of up-to-date examples and clear diagrams. These help to illustrate very effectively some of the key issues included in modern-day operations management.

The book should prove to be particularly useful for students studying for:

- AQA's A level Business Studies Modules 4 and 5
- Edexcel's Units 2 and 4
- OCR's Modules 2872, 2873 and 2877

as well as VCE, HND and degree-level Business Studies courses.

Susan Grant
Series Editor

Operations
Management

Chris Vidler

Series Editor
Susan Grant
West Oxfordshire College

Heinemann Educational Publishers
Halley Court, Jordan Hill, Oxford OX2 8EJ
a division of Reed Educational & Professional Publishing Ltd

OXFORD   MELBOURNE   AUCKLAND
JOHANNESBURG   BLANTYRE   GABORONE
IBADAN   PORTSMOUTH (NH) USA   CHICAGO

Heinemann is a registered trademark of Reed Educational & Professional Publishing Ltd

Text © Chris Vidler, 2001
First published in 2001

05 04 03 02 01
10 9 8 7 6 5 4 3 2 1

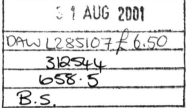
British Library Cataloguing in Publication Data
A catalogue record for this book is available from the British Library

ISBN 0 435 33225 2

Typeset and illustrated by TechType
Printed and bound by Biddles Ltd

Acknowledgements
The publishers would like to thank the following for permission to reproduce copyright
material:

AQA for the questions on pp. 90, 101–2 (AQA examination questions are reproduced by
permission of the Assessment and Qualification Alliance); Edexcel Foundation for the
questions on pp. 67, 80, 112–14; The *Financial Times* for articles on pp. 39, 50; The
Independent Syndication for the article on p. 26; The Institute of Petroleum for the map
on page 46; The OCR for questions on pp. 28–9, 42–3, 54–5 (reproduced with the kind
permission of the OCR); © Times Newspapers for the *Sunday Times* article on pp. 54–5.

The publishers have made every effort to contact copyright holders. However, if any
material has been incorrectly acknowledged, the publishers would be pleased to correct
this at the earliest opportunity.

Tel: 01865 888058
www.heinemann.co.uk

Introduction

This introduction has been produced in two parts. The first part offers guidance on how you might use this work to be a more successful student of business studies and the second part is devoted to a brief introduction to the contents of the rest of the book.

Helping you Become a More Successful Student

This book has been written to introduce you to operations management. This is a key business function and one that is often overlooked in comparison with say the external environment or financial management and control. It is seen as less 'sexy' than marketing and even less accessible or interesting as human resource management, but businesses which neglect their operations management function are likely to fail. This applies equally to the private and public sectors as it does to sales maximizing or not-for-profit organizations. Reading and understanding the concepts in this book should help you appreciate the crucial importance of operations management and reinforce the importance of how inter-related business functions are.

Operations Management has been written to supplement standard business texts, and also to provide an introduction for those studying business in higher education or for professional examinations. This means that the concepts developed and used might at first sight appear more difficult and challenging for students on AS, and Advanced GCE and VCE programmes. However, this book will help those of you going for top grades, assist in the production of high quality course work, and provide an opportunity to develop key skills. The remainder of this introduction has been written to provide and provide advice and guidance of how it might be used by students on different courses followed by a brief introduction to its contents

Using Operations Management

This book has been written to:

- help you get a better grades in your AS and Advanced Level GCE, VCE and Key Skills examinations
- stimulate and challenge students in schools, colleges and universities to think critically and analytically about Business Studies.

1

Getting a better grade

Students on VCE and GCE programmes can improve their grades by doing better in examinations and in course work. Key Skills now provide an opportunity to boost your points score on your UCAS application form. Business Studies provides lots of opportunities to generate evidence for your Key Skills Portfolio.

Examinations

Operations Management forms part of the compulsory elements of all of awarding body specifications for the new AS, Advanced and VCE business courses. Course questions on operations management come up in AQA's Units 2 and 5, OCR's Modules 2872 and 2877, and Edexcel's Unit 2. Those of you taking VCE courses will deal with operations management in Units 1 and 6. Examinations on business courses tend to have two features in common. Firstly, those students who do well need to be able to demonstrate that they understand the interrelatedness of business functions. Thus, a good student takes every opportunity to show that she or he knows that a marketing decision will have financial implications. Similarly, a student who fails to demonstrate that knowing about operations management is integral to an overall understanding of business activity will not score highly. This book reflects this aspect of the subject and is designed to help you develop these overarching skills which will be rewarded by higher grades.

Higher grades are also awarded to those students who show the ability to analyze and evaluate rather than simply describe. This book is designed to help you improve these higher order skills. There is considerable emphasis placed on modelling and the use of conceptual tools to analyze and explain business behaviour. Concepts, like critical path analysis, which many students traditionally find difficult, are carefully built up and every effort is made to illustrate with examples taken from current business practice and problems. However, you may find that this book is more challenging than more general introductory texts. No apologies are made for this, especially as the new Advanced level courses are considered by many to be harder and more demanding that those courses they have replaced.

Each chapter ends with samples of both essay style work and sample data responses questions taken mostly from the specifications for the new business examinations. If you understand the text that precedes the questions these examination challenges should be easy to overcome.

Coursework

Coursework requirements vary between different specifications. Two thirds of assessments for those of you on VCE courses are for portfolio work, whereas the assessment of GCE students is more strongly weighted to examinations. Coursework requirements for both specifications provide an opportunity to push up your grades. You should find *Operations Management* particularly helpful providing concepts and approaches that allow you to model the production function of businesses. You might research this and use it for coursework. Where you have a free choice of topics, you might like to consider a close examination of how particular organizations tackle quality issues. Similarly, you may wish to look at stock control and just-in-time. The chapters in *Operations Management* will provide you with a good basis for the 'theoretical' treatment of these topics and also give you ideas on how you might apply them to other businesses.

Key Skills

If you are a student in an FE College, you have to do key skills. Most of those of you in schools will also have to produce portfolio evidence of your competence in Application of Number, Communications and IT. You can use operations management as a springboard to develop evidence to meet the requirements of all three key skills. For example:

- You may wish to investigate how a number of particular organizations uses statistical techniques to assure quality, or to control stocks.

- Communications evidence can be generated by investigations and presentations as to how and why particular businesses are located where they are.

- The actual and potential use of IT to monitor and control the production process could provide you with a substantial and complex activity in reconciling production schedules to variations in demand.

Thinking Critically About Business

Many of you will go on to study business and related subjects at university and to apply your understanding of business when working for organizations in the private, public and voluntary sectors. This book has been written to prepare you for further study and application of operations management techniques. End of chapter references and websites have been carefully chosen to introduce you into the academic and professional world of operations management. This part of business studies may lack the glamour of topics such as marketing, and may be considered by some to be less important than financial control and management, but all businesses have to find effective ways of managing operations. One clear message of this book is that businesses failing to address operations management functions will themselves fail. Hence, the importance of the concepts introduced in this book not just for examination success, but also for your possible academic and business career.

Finally, it should be clear to the reader that this book takes a critical stance in its examination of current business practice. It includes examples and problems faced by all types of organizations. It does not accept the premise that private sector or business led solutions are the best solutions, nor does it reject such strategies as socially harmful or divisive. All organizations need to have regard to operations management decisions as evidenced by current debates about rail and air safety. Finally, the last final two chapters address issues around the vital concept of quality. They will engage you in the crucial discourse required to contribute to the development of strategies. These strategies may indeed provide long-term assurance that the UK economy becomes more competitive in the emerging global economy.

Chapter Summaries

Although you can dip into particular sections of *Operations Management*, you should try to read it from beginning to end over a short stretch of time. This will give you an overview of this business function. The book has been written to build on key concepts explained in the early chapters and then developed and applied in a number of different contexts. Some concepts may be harder to take in and understand on first reading. Make a note of any that you find particularly challenging and try a second slower reading of those sections. If you are still faced with difficulties, ask for help from your teacher, lecturer, or tutor.

The first chapter is devoted to an explanation of the input-output approach to the modelling of the transformation process which is at the heart of operations management. This may sound particularly theoretical, but this model is both easy to understand and very useful in understanding how businesses actually work.

Chapter 2 develops this model and involves consideration of different types of operations management. These include Eastern business approaches including just-in-time, continuous improvement and zero defects which have had a significant impact on traditional approaches to operations management.

Chapter 3 is devoted to various aspects of costs, including the identification of variable and fixed costs which underpins the development of break-even analysis to establish to lowest level of sales necessary to avoid making a loss. Other costing methods and concepts such as economies of scale are also considered.

Location decisions are in Chapter 4. This develops an understanding of the interdependence of locational factors including historical accident and inertia.

Chapter 5 is devoted to an examination of planning and controlling decisions faced by all organizations. This is importamt as they all have to find ways of reconciling changes and fluctuations in demand to production capacity and flexibility.

Project management techniques are examined in Chapter 6 with an emphasis on critical path analysis which is a powerful tool which is used to both plan and control projects and a favourite of examiners.

Chapter 7 is devoted to the management of inventory, more commonly known as stock control. The inability to properly control and manage stocks is a major cause of business failure.

Modern and traditional approaches to quality are considered in Chapter 8. Modern approaches such as TQM are compared to more traditional approaches which emphasize a trade off between quality and cost.

Chapter 9 is also devoted to quality, but has been written to introduce students into the important contemporary debate within business about how to best raise quality standards. This involves consideration of Japanese developed business practice, alongside an introduction to how some of the long-term failings of British industry might be best addressed.

Finally, there is a brief conclusion which seeks to draw together the principal findings of the book and answer some of the questions posed by this introduction.

Good luck.

Chapter One

Operations management defined

All organizations have to make operations management decisions, yet this is often the least understood and most neglected aspect of business studies.

Operations management (OM) refers to the way in which organizations produce goods and services. All businesses produce either goods or services. All have to manage this function, and this book is concerned with the tasks, issues and decisions that have to be made within all organizations. The first chapter examines:

- the function of operations management within organizations
- how the **input–output** model can be used to understand and explore the **transformation process**
- **buffering**
- different types of production
- functions within operations management.

All organizations have to make operations management decisions, yet this is often the least understood and most neglected aspect of business studies.

Operations management within organizations

Although operations management is concerned with decisions about the production of goods or services which is central to the existence of an organization, it is not the only or even the most important function. In addition to operations management, all organizations share six other key functions:

- marketing
- finance
- research and development
- personnel
- purchasing
- technical.

There is great variation between organizations as to how these functions are actually carried out, and that particularly applies to operations management. In some organizations this will include all the activities that are even loosely linked to production, while in others operations management will be defined much more narrowly, to exclude activities shared with other functions. These different approaches to operations management are illustrated in Figure 1.

In Figure 1(a), operations management touches upon other functions of an organization but is probably limited to the actual production of a product in service. Figure 1(b) illustrates an organization which attaches much greater importance to operations management, as it includes research and development (R&D), a significant proportion of the personnel function, and a large amount of the finance function.

Irrespective of whether or not a particular organization follows the broad or narrow definition of operations management, the diagram represents differing proportions of raw materials, information, plant/machinery and employees.

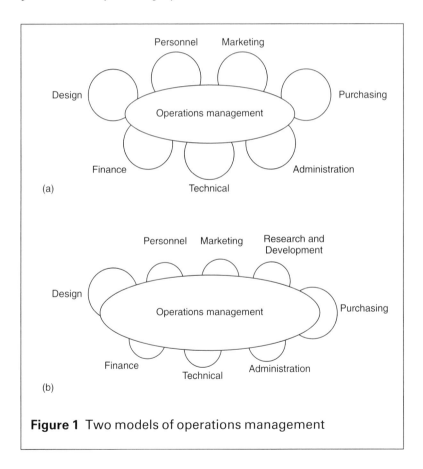

Figure 1 Two models of operations management

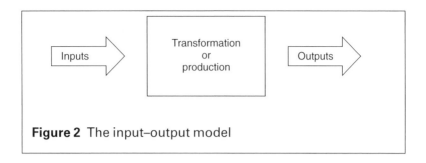

Figure 2 The input–output model

The central box in Figure 2 represents the actual process of transformation which leads to the output of goods or services. This very simple model can provide a very powerful means of understanding and analysing how organizations actually work. It can be applied to all businesses irrespective of the form of their outputs. The examples which follow illustrate the ease with which this model can be applied.

- *Cybercandy.* Cybercandy is a newly established internet-based business which sells sweets from around the world to customers. They are very much a service-based industry. They buy and store different sweets, have invested in producing an attractive and user-friendly website, and take pride in trying to ensure that their products reach customers within two working days of an order being placed. The transformation involves getting products from all over the world to customers who can also be located all over the world. This can be modelled as shown in Figure 3.

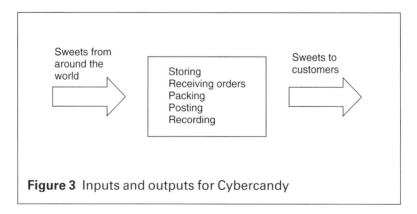

Figure 3 Inputs and outputs for Cybercandy

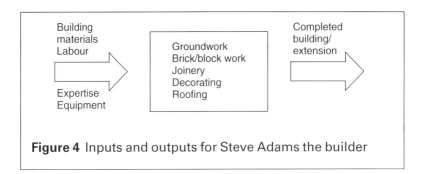

Figure 4 Inputs and outputs for Steve Adams the builder

- *Steve Adams the builder.* Steve runs his own building business and takes on all kinds of building work. The main materials he uses are blocks, timber, sand and cement. He uses his skills and sometimes the help of a labourer to transform these materials into extensions, drains, walls and houses. This is depicted in Figure 4.

- *SCA Packaging.* SCA is a Swedish-owned multinational company which amongst other outputs produces packaging materials for a range of industrial customers. The transformation process is far more complex than in the other examples. There is a series of stages by which timber is grown, harvested, pulped, turned into card, printed, cut and shaped to meet customers' specifications. All this is depicted in Figure 5.

Inputs

As illustrated above, inputs usually take three forms:

- materials
- information
- customers' specifications.

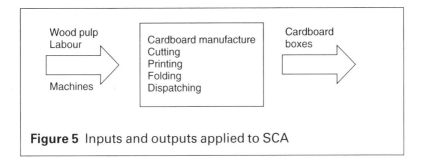

Figure 5 Inputs and outputs applied to SCA

The relative proportions are likely to vary according to the type of business or organization in question. Thus, while a hairdresser will input materials in the form of water, shampoo and energy, and some degree of information processing (especially in respect of particular fashions), his or her main activity will be making customers feel better about themselves. The biggest single substance used by a brewery will be water, which along with hops, yeast and barley malt will ensure that materials are the most important input. Operations like electricity supply (not generation) will be dominated by information processing, recording the usage of individual customers, and staying on top of the billing process.

Transformation

The nature of the transformation process will be closely related to the particular form and relative importance of the inputs. Traditional manufacturing involves changing the physical properties of materials. Thus, SCA uses machines to change squishy, formless wood pulp into strong semi-durable cardboard boxes.

Information processing is increasingly associated with the use of ICT to automate and speed up the ability of organizations to handle and transform data. This is well illustrated by the radical changes that are affecting the nature of the banking and insurance industries.

Finally, customer or people processing is likely to be the most labour-intensive form of the transformation. Those industries in which this is most important, such as catering, hospitality and healthcare, are likely to be major employers.

Output

A crude distinction can be made between outputs of things that can be seen, touched, stored and used – for example cars, baked beans and computers – and things that do not have these qualities – services such as those provided by the education, entertainment and transportation industries.

However, it is increasingly hard for businesses producing goods to survive if they ignore the service element contained within their product. Car, computer, even machine-tool manufacturers invest heavily to try to ensure that customers associate their products with quality, and high levels of customer care. Similarly, football clubs and rock stars may be providing a service in the form of entertainment, but they gain greater revenues and market penetration by 'merchandizing' certain (often over-priced) goods.

Input–output modelling of operations within an organization

The input–output model of the transformation process can also be used to analyse operations within an organization. Most operations consist of a number of sub-units, sections or departments. Thus a typical supermarket will involve warehousing/delivery, shelf stacking, checkout, inventory control, and cash-handling functions, each with a particular input and output. Similarly, the process involved in the manufacture of cardboard packing cases consists of transforming card into sheets, cutting, printing and folding. This is illustrated in Figure 6.

Some organizations, like the BBC, have used this type of analysis in an attempt to increase efficiencies by creating a series of **internal markets**, whereby each function buys its inputs from other functions and sells it on to other functions. Thus 'Props' buys in costumes, stage sets and the like and sells them on to 'Production', who have the responsibility of putting individual programmes together.

Buffering

This is the term used to describe measures which can be taken to insulate organizations or departments within organizations from variations in the supply of inputs and the provision of outputs. Stocks of raw materials, partly finished goods and finished goods are kept and can be drawn upon if there is any disruption in the supply of inputs or in production itself. This process of buffering is illustrated in Figure 7.

Buffering can also be used to even out irregularities in the supply of inputs used by service providers. Thus many organizations, from doctors to dentists to ticket sellers to retailers, make or expect customers to queue. Their services are not offered the moment they are requested by customers. Buyers are expected to wait in line for their turn to be served. This form of buffering enables the organization to save on resources devoted to dealing with customers. For example, a

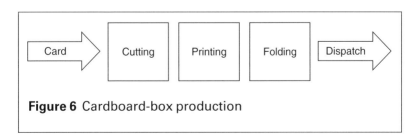

Figure 6 Cardboard-box production

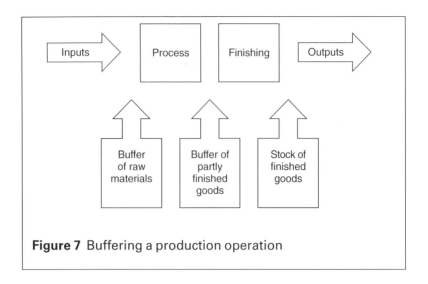

Figure 7 Buffering a production operation

supermarket which expects customers to queue to pay for their goods will need fewer checkouts.

There are costs associated with buffering. Moreover, modern operations management strategies see the practice as a source of inefficiency within organizations. These issues are explored in Chapter 7.

Different types of production

Although the use and application of the input–output model emphasizes the similarities between operations management in different organizations, there are significant differences between different operations. Four measures can be used to emphasize variations in operations management. They are:

- **volume of output**
- **variety of output**
- variations in demand
- customer contact.

Volume of output

This is often measured in terms of output per day/shift/hour/minute. High-volume production like pressing CDs, processing customers at theme parks or producing Tetra packs of Ribena are all characterized by highly specialized, highly standardized, high-speed processes which are usually very highly mechanized or automated, and often associated with low unit costs of production.

Alternatively, the production of custom- or hand-made clothing, running a specialist restaurant, or making Morgan cars are all slower, more labour-intensive operations which involve less specialization, less mechanization and higher unit costs.

Variety of output

Goods that are mass produced tend to be characterized by fewer variations. Although car manufacturers may try to promote variety by incorporating different engine sizes and levels of specification, there is not much variety in the production of individual models. Indeed, the same factory in Portugal currently produces almost identical 'people carriers' for different companies – the VW Sharon, the Seat Alhambra and the Ford Galaxy. Similarly, if you want to take an underground train from one side of London to another, the only variety you are likely to find is different waiting times at different times of the day.

More specialized and low-volume operations are more likely to be characterized by variety. Weddings and funerals can be tailored to meet the differing needs of different customers. The production of such goods and services has to be flexible, but the price of greater variety is likely to be higher unit costs.

Variations in demand

This relates more directly to patterns which may be beyond the direct control of the producer.

Customer demand for some products and services can show both predictable and unpredictable variations. It is hard for retail clothing outlets to predict the demand for particular styles and fashions. The demand for many products, not just ice-cream and beer, changes according to the weather.

Such variations in demand place particular pressures on businesses. They need to be able to respond flexibly to changes in demand, but there are limits and costs to ensuring that the operations match outputs with demand. For example, if sufficient staff are employed to cope with peaks in demand, there will be times when there is insufficient work for them all, thereby forcing up unit costs.

On the other hand, when demand is stable and predictable it is far easier to match outputs to demand as efficiently as possible. Waste is minimized and unit costs will be lower. Fewer variations in demand occur with basic foodstuffs like bread and milk, and with services such as commuter transport in urban areas.

Customer contact

Production processes are often invisible to customers. Few consumers ever set foot in factories, so employees have no need for highly developed customer-care skills. Internet-based businesses and other forms of direct selling deliberately limit customer contact as a way of keeping customer care costs to a minimum. Other operations involve high levels of customer contact by their very nature. It would be hard to be a doctor without any patients.

Most organizations probably combine functions which have a high level of customer contact with those with much less. The differences between the public areas of retail outlets and the 'back-office' functions are often stark. High levels of customer friendliness in showrooms and in selling areas often provide a contrast to the stark, functional nature of store and stock rooms and the more informal behaviour of the workers within these departments.

Functions within operations management

Figure 1 provided an initial indication of the functions likely to be found within operations management. They include R&D, technical, purchasing, personnel, some aspects of marketing and some aspects of finance. In addition, there are activities which link each of the above strategically, in terms of:

- an overall organizational strategy
- an **operations strategy**.

Each of the functions and activities mentioned above is outlined in this final section of the chapter. The rest of this book is devoted to helping to develop a better understanding of all these functions and the over-arching and linking strategic considerations which will help determine the business performance of any organization.

Research and development

Operations management in most organizations will include a responsibility for R&D. This will apply particularly to finding ways of making existing production and provision of services more cost-effective, the modification of existing products and services, and the development of new products and services. The importance attached to this function will depend upon two key factors:

- the degree of competition within the market in question
- the particular ethos and culture of the organization.

For example, the retail grocery market is highly competitive, with Tesco having the largest market share. This company is aggressive and dynamic and is continually trying to gain greater market share at the expense of its competitors. Tesco spends a significant proportion of its annual budget on its R&D function. Other businesses operating in less competitive markets are more likely to be less dynamic and innovative, and will devote a smaller proportion of their budget to research and development.

Technical

This function involves all the processes that are involved in the actual production of a good or service. They need to be coordinated, efficient and smooth-running. For example, an ordinary photocopier consists of hundreds of different components. The technical function requires that each of these be produced to particular quality standards, at a particular place, at a particular time. Similarly the work of a builder is essentially technical – deciding on how particular jobs should be tackled.

In a service-oriented organization such as McDonald's the technical function is equally important. Each Big Mac is meant to be produced and supplied to the same critical standards irrespective of where it is sold. This means that people with 'Mcjobs' have very clearly defined and repetitive routines to follow to ensure that they fit in with highly specialized technical systems of how to produce and sell hamburgers and related products in a particular way.

Purchasing

This is a rather unglamorous but essential function in any organization. Inputs of resources have to be obtained from somewhere. Quality standards and delivery deadlines need to be met, and above all costs need to be minimized. The globalization of markets means that materials and components can be obtained or sourced from anywhere in the world. A business which fails to adapt and change its purchasing to take account of this risks losing competitive advantage, as Marks & Spencer and a number of other famous companies have discovered to their cost.

Personnel

Whereas the management of employees is often considered to be a human resource function, the day-to-day supervision and motivation of employees will often be an operations management function. In a traditionally organized factory, individual workers will probably report directly to a foreman or supervisor who will then report to a works or departmental manager. Such operations managers might also be given responsibility for the recruitment and training of staff. The fact that many managers have themselves little human resource management training orfew highly developed interpersonal skills is often a source of tension within organizations.

Marketing and finance

These would not normally be considered to be operations management functions. However, all business activity and decision-making is interrelated.

Business books and the real world of business contain many examples of companies which fail because of poor communication and poor relations between marketing and either operations management or finance, or in the worst cases between all three functions. Salesmen who promise deliveries of what it is technically impossible to produce, or production teams who make products for which there is no market, or have no understanding of the costing of particular processes, provide recipes for business disaster – hence the importance of marketing, finance and other functions to operations management.

Overall organizational strategy

It follows from the above that efficient and effective operations management requires a clear understanding of the overall strategic objectives of the organization. A clear vision is required of what the organization is setting out to achieve. This is not necessarily as easy to do as it is to say, especially in large organizations in which individual managers and directors have high levels of autonomy. Much will depend upon internal organization and the vision and leadership qualities of the managing director, or whoever has overall responsibility for the business.

Operations strategy

Finally, the function of operations strategy refers to the translation of overall strategic objectives into particular operational objectives. While these are likely to differ between organizations, for the reasons outlined in this chapter, all operations managers have to strive to achieve quality standards, to meet deadlines and to respond flexibly to customers – all within cost or budget constraints.

KEY WORDS	
Operations management	Internal markets
Input–output	Volume of output
Transformation process	Variety of output
Buffering	Operations strategy

Further reading
Galloway, R., *Principles of Operations Management*, Routledge, 1993.
Harding, H., *Production/Operations Management*, Pitman, 1992.
Hill, T., *The Essence of Operations Management*, Prentice Hall, 1991.
Wild, R., *Production and Operations Management*, Cassell, 1990.

Useful websites
Bized: www.bized.ac.uk/ (an excellent introduction to business sites)
Bized: www.bized.ac.uk/virtual/cb/factory/production/intro1.htm (takes viewers inside a balloon-making factory)
Bized: www.bized.ac.uk/compfact/boots/cases1.htm (operations management at Boots)
St Mary's University: www.engr.stmarytx.edu/manufacturing/qm. htm (online tests of the viewer's understanding of manufacturing processes)
TOMI: www.members.tripod.co.uk/tomi/cases.html (one of the best UK-based portals, aimed at university students, but probably the most useful Internet resource currently available)

Activity
Choose an organization with which you are familiar and analyze how it undertakes the function of operations management. Use the input–output model to explain how inputs are transformed into outputs. Identify the key factors affecting how operations management is organized, and assess the relative importance attached to the individual operations management functions.

Data response question

Read the following brief passage which provides information about a major company involved in the ever-changing world of computers and toys. After reading about the company, Character Group PLC, answer the two questions that follow on the next page.

Character Group PLC changes policy

The business world is a world of constant change. Companies can experience significant shifts in demand for their products, changes in their costs and the rise of new competitors.

Companies that are involved in the toy and computer industries are particularly subject to changes. This is primarily because advances in information technology are constantly changing the design and capacity of computers. Toys, of course, are subject to seasonal changes in demand, with peak sales being at Christmas time. Toys are also increasingly linked in with films, TV programmes and pop bands.

One company that has recently had to adapt to a changing market is the Character Group PLC.

The company is involved in a wide range of products and business activities including the design, development and international distribution and sale of branded and character-licensed toys, watches, clocks, giftware, toiletries, stationery and computer accessories. Among its products and licences are Chicken Run, Britney Spears Dolls, Pokemon and Mr Men.

The Group comprises three divisions – the Toy Division, Gifts, Stationery and Toiletry Division and the Overseas Division. The last division is made up of World Wide Licences and Delta Millennium Far East, which distributes WWL's computer accessories.

In 1999, the company ran into difficulties with its Star Wars related products. The company had anticipated a very high demand for the products following the release of the Star Wars film, but this did not materialize.

As a result, the company decided to reduce the overall stocks and sought to improve efficiency and cut costs. It also expanded its product base and announced its intention to work closely with customers. The aims behind this strategy included meeting the needs of its customers more effectively and taking greater advantage of the opportunities for, and development of e-commerce and electronic trading.

(a) What are the similarities between Character Group PLC and Cybercandy? [5 marks]

(b) Discuss the possible benefits and costs of cutting down on stocks. [6 marks]

(c) Discuss whether the Toy Division of Character Group PLC is likely to be involved mainly in high or low volume operations. [4 marks]

(d) Explain why close contact with customers is important for the development of e-commerce. [4 marks]

(e) Discuss two ways a company could cuts its costs. [6 marks]

Chapter Two

Types of processing of goods and services

The input–output model can be used to model the transformation processes involved in any business organization. It is a simple yet powerful tool which can yield insight and understanding of operations management processes and decisions.

This chapter focuses on the transformation process identified in the input–output model outlined in the previous chapter – see Figure 2 on page 6. Consideration is given to the classification of different processing methods in the manufacture of goods. These are related to two key operations management factors: *volume* and *variety* of outputs. Finally, an introduction is made to the significance of lean production on traditional operations management models.

The input–output model can be used to model the transformation processes involved in any business organization. It is a simple yet powerful tool which can yield insight and understanding of operations management processes and decisions.

The provision of goods

The process types for the provision of goods are (see Figure 8):

- **project**
- **jobbing**
- **batch**
- **mass**
- **continuous** (or flow).

A similar typology can be applied to service operations:

- project
- batch
- mass.

Project processes

Project processes are typically associated with the production of one-off projects. For example, shipbuilding companies will compete with one another to tender for the order of a particular design of warship,

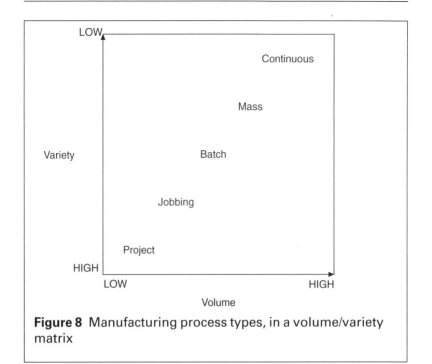

Figure 8 Manufacturing process types, in a volume/variety matrix

bulk carrier or drilling platform. Projects such as these usually take a long time to complete, will be highly individualized to the needs of the customer, and will probably require the application of special skills and technologies which only a few companies may possess. For these reasons the volume of production is likely to be low, but the producers will be able to incorporate a high level of variety in terms of final outputs.

Jobbing processes

Jobbing processes, too, are concerned with producing one-off products to meet the needs of individual customers, but the volume of production is likely to be higher than with project processes. For example, a pump manufacturer can produce a basic product that can be modified to undertake many different processes. Additional features can be added or taken away to enable the individual demands of customers to be met. Nonetheless the pump maker, printer or balloon manufacturer will specialize in undertaking a series of specific processes which can be combined together to produce a relatively high variety of outcomes. The manufacturer undertaking jobbing processes is likely to use multi-purpose machinery and employ workers who are both skilled and versatile in what they do.

Batch processes

With batch processing the degree of variety is reduced and the volume of production is likely to be increased. For example, many food producers will produce batches of similar products for a variety of customers. Some batches may differ only according to branding, while others will contain different proportions of key ingredients. This form of processing is becoming more and more common as customers demand greater variety in terms of what they buy, and companies continually strive to sell products which are differentiated from those of their competitors. Efficient batch production requires quick change times between different production runs, which necessitates the use of sophisticated multi-tasking machinery and flexible multi-skilled workers.

Mass production

Mass production is synonymous with the production line, on which products containing a limited range of variation can be produced in high volume. Henry Ford is credited with introducing this type of manufacturing process to the production of automobiles in the United States in the 1920s. He produced a highly standardized product, and by simplifying the production processes each task could be broken down into its simplest and most efficient form. This makes mass production repetitive and predictable, which in turn results in boring jobs for many workers, or a justification for investment in different forms of robotic production.

Continuous or flow production

This form of processing takes mass production one step further. Some products like petrol, beer and paper are so uniform (i.e. contain so little variation) that they can be produced continuously. Crude oil is pumped from the North Sea directly to the Grangemouth refinery and turned into a variety of products including petrol and diesel fuel, which we then pumped almost continuously into tankers for distribution in Scotland and the north of England. It is a continuous process that is highly automated, which requires enormous investment in plant and machinery and which employs few workers.

One version of flow production is cell production. This involves breaking down a continuous flow production line into self-contained units, each with a team of workers. The advantage claimed for this method is that workers receive more job satisfaction from working with a small group of colleagues and on a specific 'completed' part of the production process.

The provision of services

Services can also be differentiated according to volume/variety characteristics, and a simple typology can be used to classify three (sometimes overlapping) process types (see Figure 9).

Project services

Service activities that are dedicated to meeting the particular needs of individual customers come closest to fitting in this category. Accountants, solicitors, auditors and organizations of professionals are usually highly focused and responsive to clients' needs. Within their particular professional field, each organization would be expected to deal with one-off situations, requiring the employment of specialist staff and high levels of interpersonal skills. Some projects might be for an extended period of time, leading to a low volume of output.

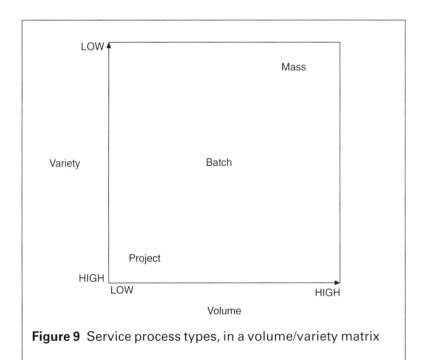

Figure 9 Service process types, in a volume/variety matrix

Batch services

This term can be applied to a wide range of service operations. Banks, insurance companies and rental businesses tend to offer consumers a clearly defined range of services that can be modified to meet some of the needs of individual customers. For example, each high street bank offers a limited range of banking accounts, insurance, share dealing and foreign exchange services. There may be front- and back-office specialists in each field, and the limited variation offered should allow efficient and quick responses to customer demands, leading to a relatively high volume of 'output'.

Mass services

Mass services involve less variation and higher volume and are increasingly characterized by automated processes like cash machines or operations handled by call centres. They also include retailing, where the emphasis is on reducing queuing and ensuring the rapid processing of customers' requirements.

Choosing the right process

It follows from the foregoing descriptions that an individual business should consider the following in deciding which of the different ways of organizing operations is most appropriate.

- High-volume processes should enable businesses to reduce unit costs and therefore become more competitive.
- High-volume outputs are often associated with heavy investment in computer-aided and controlling processes.
- High-volume production can result in a trade-off between cutting unit costs and meeting the particular needs of individual customers (i.e. varying the outputs).
- The development of more flexible technologies and multi-skilling of workers has enabled some businesses to reconcile the benefits of high-volume production with customer demands for greater product and service differentiation.

Lean production

From the 1960s, Japanese-owned businesses gained significant shares in markets which Europeans and North Americans traditionally regarded as their own. Sales of lightweight motorbikes, cars and a wide range of electrical goods and computers became increasingly dominated by Japanese and Far Eastern producers. For a long time the success of these businesses was ignored, but in the early 1980s there was a flood of publications and research which advocated Japanese ways of organizing not just operations management but also all business functions.

Lean production

Lean production is the term that has been used to capture new ways of organizing production. The essence of the concept is that organizations should aim to eliminate all forms of waste. In terms of the transformation process, the costs of production are minimized while the value of outputs is maximized.

The concept of waste is all-powerful, ranging from the elimination of outputs which do not sell, for whatever reason, to ensuring that stores are minimized and that the full creative abilities of all workers are maximized. The advocates of lean production focus on three aspects:

- just-in-time
- continuous improvement
- zero defects.

Each of these is considered in greater detail in the chapters which follow. However, their significance is such that it is useful to have an overview of what each might mean in relation to the processes associated with operations management.

Just-in-time

'Just-in-time' means what it says – managing all operations within an organization to ensure that materials are received or sales are delivered *exactly* when they are needed, not before. The application of this principle is to eliminate the waste that is associated with holding buffer stocks of raw materials, partly finished goods and final goods (look back to Figure 7 on page 10). It is argued that holding buffer stocks not only ties up working capital (another source of waste) but also insulates the different stages of the production process from knowing whether or not problems exist in other stages of production.

However, for just-in-time production to work, certain key requirements need to be satisfied:

- *Quality*. This is crucial. If a company involved in mass production has adopted just-in-time working, its assembly processes will be halted if components fail to meet minimum specification requirements.

- *Speed*. If orders are to be met directly from production, operations will have to be undertaken quickly in order to meet customer requirements.

The just-in-time economy

HAMISH MCRAE

Much has been made of the just-in-time economy in the US. The argument is that companies carry much lower stocks than they used to, thanks largely to improvements in information technology. Since every three months their results are scrutinised by the markets they are also under ever greater pressure to match any fall-off in demand by immediately cutting costs. The sharpness of the current fall in the US economy is being attributed to decisions taken in December when the first signs of a slow-down appeared. It is being argued (rightly or wrongly) that the cuts in US interest rates now will encourage companies to be more optimistic in March when they make decisions about the next quarter …

Independent, 2 February 2001

- *Reliability*. Similarly, if suppliers of materials, or the operation of machines or workers, cannot be fully relied upon at all times, problems will occur and production will be halted, whereas the existence of buffer stocks would ensure that production continued.

- *Flexibility*. Switching from the production of one batch to another has to be achieved smoothly with as little 'down time' as possible; hence the need for both workers and machines to be as flexible as possible.

Continuous improvement

Continuous improvement is usually associated with 'total quality management' (TQM). It involves an approach to improving operations management by all employees, with both managers and process workers constantly striving to find better and more efficient ways of producing a product or providing a service. As explained more fully in Chapters 8 and 9, this can involve radically changing employer–employee relationships in order to create a corporate culture in which all feel secure enough to participate and contribute.

This strategy is eastern in its origins. It can be contrasted with traditional western approaches emphasizing the improvement of operations management through major changes – which might be associated with organizational restructuring or investment in different production technologies.

Zero defects

Another revolutionary change in operations management thinking, again associated with eastern business practice and related to both continuous improvement and just-in-time, is the notion of 'zero defects'.

As will be explained in Chapters 8 and 9, traditional approaches to quality control tolerated the production or supply of some sub-standard products or services. Although tolerance levels might be imposed at a very high level, it can be argued that the very acceptance of any defective outputs from the transformation process legitimizes poor quality. It has also been argued that traditional approaches to operations management actually undervalue the *costs* of poor quality.

Designing and managing operations management to ensure zero defects is likely to result in different practices, procedures and management–employee relationships than would be the case when some level of defect is tolerated.

KEY WORDS

Project	Lean production
Jobbing	Just-in-time
Batch	Continuous improvement
Mass	Zero defects
Continuous	

Further reading

Galloway, R., *Principles of Operations Management*, Routledge, 1993.

Harding, H., *Production/Operations Management*, Pitman, 1992.

Jewell, B., *An Integrated Approach to Business Studies*, Longman, 2000.

Wild, R., *Production and Operations Management*, Cassell, 1990.

Useful websites

Bized: www.bized.ac.uk/virtual/cb/factory/production/worksheets2.htm (describes various production methods)

Bized: www.bized.ac.uk/compfact/bae/bae8.htm (examples of how BA Systems organize production)

Essay topic

Assess the impact of technological change on the choice of the most appropriate operations methods. Support your arguments by reference to specific industries.

Data response question

This task is based on part of an OCR Business Studies specimen paper issued in 2000. Read the piece below and look over the tables on the next page before answering the question. [25 marks]

The Wilson Trucking Company

The Wilson Trucking Company (WTC) has been in business for almost a century, producing a wide variety of long- and short-haulage trucks. The firm is one of the largest in the industry, employing some 500 workers on a site just off the A1 south of Newcastle.

The WTC produces between 10 and 14 trucks per week, the average time it takes to build a truck being about 1100 labour-hours. Trucks are generally in the firm's workshop for seven weeks, which represents a large amount of tied-up capital.

The firm currently uses a mixture of cell and job production methods. The bought-in chassis are worked upon in cells which have a team of four workers who build the truck's outer framework. Once this stage is complete the chassis is rolled into the spraying area where it is given a basic coat of rust-proofing. From there it returns to its cell where the basic structure of the driver cabin and storage facilities are worked upon. Once this is complete, it passes through a number of departments where seating, lighting and the more specialized features are added. These range from freezing facilities for the transportation of food, to canisters required to convey toxic and caustic substances. New customer demands never cease to amaze the firm, and increasingly it has had to adapt to the changing market needs. Once the storage facilities are installed, the truck is painted to the customer's specifications. From there, it is sent to the inspection department where it is examined thoroughly for any defects. Frequently, a fault sheet is issued and the truck has to be reworked in some way or another.

The issue of quality control has been a problem for some time at the WTC, especially as it has recently delayed some customer delivery dates. The inspection department has alienated the rest of the plant as it is perceived that the department is looking to fail every truck it inspects. The number of faults recorded over the last month are shown in Table A.

The firm uses a variety of stock-control methods depending upon the particular component. The WTC has developed a strong partnership with its chassis supplier and has now come to rely on just one firm. For the high-volume low-value products, such as nuts and bolts, a visual Kan Ban system is used – this is operated by the supplier who visits the factory to ensure that supplies do not run too low. The more specialized components such as toxic canister tanks are ordered to a just-in-time system; this is used because frequently customers ask for very specific features. The suppliers for these components are located near London. Other components, such as headlights and paint, are ordered through a computer-generated CAM system – the firm being able to predict demand for these products using a standard formula based upon usage and lead times (refer to Table B for further details).

Table A Summary of faults recorded

	Number of vehicles inspected	Number of minor faults recorded	Number of major faults recorded	Number of labour-hours required to rectify faults
Week 1	12	5	3	20
Week 2	14	23	2	18
Week 3	13	17	1	16
Week 4	11	7	4	34

Table B Summary of the WTC stock ordering situation

	Chassis	High-volume low-value components	Specialized components	General items (e.g. paint, headlights)
Lead time	4 weeks	1 day	6 weeks	3 days
Minimum stock kept	0	2500 components (I day's average usage)	0	75 items (5 days' average usage)
Maximum stock	0	2500 components (I day's average usage)	0	105 items (7 days' average usage)
Average price of each component	£20 000	20p	£38 000	£15

1. The production method used by the WTC is under review. The firm is considering moving from cell to flow production. Discuss this proposal, highlighting the advantages and disadvantages for:
   (a) the firm   [16 marks]
   (b) its employees.   [10 marks]

Chapter Three

Costing operations

For most organizations, the cost of operations is the largest element of total costs. To ignore the cost of operations would be an act of extreme folly for any organization.

The bottom line of any business activity is profitability, or for non-profit organizations, viability. Profitability and viability involve setting the revenues or income from any activity against the costs of the activity. For most organizations, the cost of operations is the largest element of total costs. To ignore the cost of operations would be an act of extreme folly for any organization.

There are different ways in which costs can be defined and analysed, and this chapter provides an introduction to:

- definitions of costs
- **break-even analysis**
- costing methods
- economies and diseconomies of scale.

Definitions of costs

All payments made by a business in the production of a good or provision of a service are called costs. It is useful to distinguish between overheads and running costs.

- Overheads are costs of production which businesses have to pay irrespective of their level of output. For example, a bookshop is likely to be faced with bills for rent, business rates and repayment of loans, and these will remain the same irrespective of how many books are sold. These expenditures are classified as **fixed costs**, and the convention is that they can be changed only when major changes are made to operations – such as when purchasing a new machine, or closing retail outlets.

- Running costs, such as payments for wages, stock purchases and the like, which will change as operations and sales change, are classified as **variable costs**.

In practice, however, it is not always easy to decide whether a particular cost should be classified as fixed or variable. For example, contracts and salaries might be agreed to cover a particular length of time, making them fixed, whereas maintenance costs might change considerably as output changes, making them variable.

The addition of fixed to variable costs gives **total costs,** which include all the costs faced by a business in the production of a good or a provision of a service.

The total cost divided by the output of the business gives the **average cost,** which is commonly referred to as the **unit cost.** This is probably the most useful of these measures as it indicates the cost of producing each item or providing a service.

The data contained in Figure 10 are based on the actual costs of running a certain bookshop. From this, it is easy to compute the monthly total cost (total variable cost plus total fixed cost) of running the bookshop (column 2 plus column 4). From this it is possible to derive the average cost of selling convenient bundles of books. In March, 2500 books were sold at this bookshop. If this figure is divided into the total costs of £8850, the average cost of selling each book is £3.54.

Doubling the sales figure in the following month would have the effects shown in Figure 11.

The total cost of selling 5000 books is now £11 850, giving an average or unit cost of £2.37. This reduction in the cost of selling each book has been achieved because the fixed costs or overheads have been spread over higher sales.

Fixed costs	£	Variable costs	£
Rent	2000	Purchase of new stock	2000
Uniform business rate	1000	Postage	300
Bank loan repayment	750	Telephone	200
Depreciation of computer and other equipment	50	Overtime	500
Insurance	50		
Wages	2000		
Total fixed cost	5850	Total variable cost	3000
Total cost £8850			

Figure 10 Average monthly costs of Forest Bookshop, March 2001

Fixed costs	£	Variable costs	£
Rent	2000	Purchase of new stock	4000
Uniform business rate	1000	Postage	600
Bank loan repayment	750	Telephone	400
Depreciation of computer and other equipment	50	Overtime	1000
Insurance	50		
Wages	2000		
Total fixed cost	5850	Total variable cost	6000
Total cost £11 850			

Figure 11 Average monthly costs of Forest Bookshop, April 2001

Break-even analysis

This technique uses the concepts outlined above – revenue, fixed costs and variable costs – to indicate the minimum level of sales which will enable costs to be covered; hence the term 'break-even'. This analysis can be undertaken by the application of a simple formula or by the construction of a break-even chart.

Break-even analysis using a formula

$$\text{Break-even number of units} = \frac{\text{fixed costs}}{\text{unit price minus variable cost per unit}}$$

Using the data for April from the Forest Bookshop, and assuming that the average book sells for £5.00, we have:

- fixed costs = £5850
- average selling price per book = £5.00
- average variable cost per book sold = 6000/5000 = 1.20

$$\text{Break-even number of units} = \frac{5850}{5.00 - 1.20} = 1539.47$$

In other words, the bookshop needs to sell 1540 books (you can't sell 0.47 of a book) each month to cover its costs. Higher sales will bring the business into profit and lower sales will generate losses.

Break-even analysis using a chart

This form of analysis is useful because it can be used to show the relationship between sales and profit (or loss) at all levels of output. The data from the Forest Bookshop can be used to produce a break-even chart by following the steps outlined below (see Figure 12).

- Sales are measured on the horizontal axis and revenue and costs on the vertical axis.
- The monthly fixed costs of £5850 in March are represented by a horizontal line.
- The variable costs are indicated as 0 when sales are 0, rising upwards to the right.
- These are added to the fixed costs to illustrate how total costs rise as sales rise.
- The revenue line is then added, again starting from 0 when sales are 0 and rising upwards to the right.

Note that revenue rises more sharply than total costs. If sales are less than 1540 (the break-even point at B), then costs are greater than revenue and a loss will be made. If sales are greater than 1540, revenue exceeds costs and profits will be made.

Sales in April were actually 5000 books, exceeding the break-even point by 3460. This difference is called the *margin of safety*.

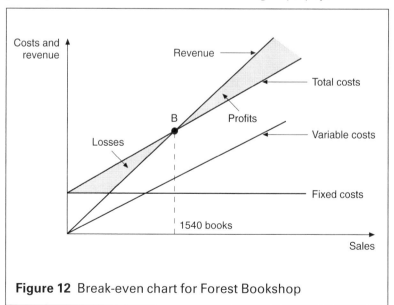

Figure 12 Break-even chart for Forest Bookshop

Finally, it should be clear that if any of the key variables – sales, fixed costs or variable costs – change this would be reflected in a new break-even point.

Other costing concepts

There are number of other costing concepts which can be used in operations management.

Marginal cost

Marginal cost is the additional cost of producing an extra unit of output of a particular good or service. For example, if a clothing manufacturing company were to produce an extra suit, it would be faced with the costs of additional materials and extra labour, but would not usually have to pay out any more for design or machine setting costs.

This concept is particularly useful in helping to decide whether a profit-making business should take on new orders. It also helps to explain why some businesses offer goods or services for sale at heavily discounted prices, particularly when fixed costs form a high proportion of total costs. For example, the additional cost incurred by carrying an extra passenger on a train or plane are minimal – just a small amount for ticketing, personal service and food or refreshments. It will pay a business to sell otherwise empty seats as long as the extra passengers pay enough to cover the variable costs they create.

Opportunity cost

Opportunity cost is a concept much used by economists. It is the cost of what has to be *sacrificed* in order to produce something or provide a service. For example, if a local authority chooses to rent out leisure facilities for a conference or similar event, it cannot at that time devote those particular resources to other uses. It might, therefore, lose revenue it would otherwise have gained from customers using its swimming or fitness facilities. The value of this lost revenue represents an 'opportunity cost' – and having an understanding of this would help the local authority decide whether or not to let out its facilities, and at what price.

Social and private costs

External costs is another concept developed and used by economists to measure the effects of business decisions on third parties. For example, the use of tobacco imposes costs on the whole community in the form of paying (through taxation) for the treatment of those who suffer from smoking-related diseases. A socially responsible organization will attempt to gauge the costs of its activities on third parties, and governments might use the existence of external costs as a reason for imposing taxes on organizations which create external costs.

A **private cost** is that which actually falls on the organization providing a particular good or service. It will be the same as the total costs considered earlier. Private costs and external costs are together referred to as **social cost** and represent the total cost to society of producing the product.

Direct and indirect costs

These are costs of particular relevance to operations management, and they are used to do costings of particular processes or services. **Direct costs** are those costs which are directly related to the production of a particular item or service. **Indirect costs** are harder to attribute in this way. This particular problem is considered in more detail in the following section.

Costing methods

As indicated in the previous section, it is often hard to work out what it actually costs to produce a particular product or provide a service. It might sound peculiar, but many organizations, especially those in the voluntary and public sectors, don't know the actual cost of providing specific services. This is especially true of large organizations providing a wide number of services.

For example, as part of its services to the community, the Environmental Health Department of the Forest of Dean District Council will investigate complaints about noise pollution, pests, dangerous dogs and a whole host of other issues. It charges for some of these services but has problems in establishing the price levels. It is straightforward enough to calculate the direct costs of dealing with a complaint about wasps, rats or other unwelcome intruders. These will include the operative's time, his or her travel costs, and the use of any equipment and materials. However, there are also indirect costs to consider: the receptionist's time in taking and dealing with the original enquiry, supervision costs in terms of scheduling jobs, record-keeping, paperwork – all should be taken into account. On top of this are all the overhead costs. Running even a small district council involves a turnover of millions and provides a considerable number of administration and management jobs.

What contribution should the customer make towards these overheads? Three different techniques can be used to address this issue.

The full-cost technique

The **full-cost technique** would be appropriate for a small business producing a limited range of goods or services, and would involve calculating the total amount of overheads and dividing by total output. An electrician fitting digital TV receivers might spend £150 a week on what he or she considered to be overheads – the cost of keeping a van on the road, some secretarial assistance, time to organize visits, keeping accounts up to date and so forth. The electrician might expect to fit 40 satellite dishes and decoders in an average week. The overhead per visit works out at 150/40 or £3.75 per visit. In order to calculate the actual or full cost of each visit, he or she needs to add £3.75 to the direct costs incurred.

This approach could be made slightly more sophisticated if the electrician were to allocate overhead expenses in direct relationship to the actual time spent on each installation.

Absorption costing

Absorption costing is a method which seeks to allocate all indirect costs more systematically, according to the nature of the individual indirect cost. Thus, a manufacturing operation with a number of assembly plants might identify three major types of indirect costs:

- human resource management, including the selection and training of workers
- depreciation and maintenance costs
- site-related costs such as heat and light, rent and business rates.

The share of each plant or profit centre of the human resource costs might be divided according to the number of workers employed in each separate facility. Depreciation and maintenance costs might be apportioned according to an accounting or book value, while site-related costs might be allocated in direct relationship to the volume or size of the individual workshops.

The idea of this approach is that all indirect costs will be allocated to individual cost centres, and this can make final pricing decisions easier. Each product line will bear both direct costs and a proportion of indirect costs, and a selling price can be established by adding on an appropriate profit margin.

This method has the advantage over full-cost approaches in that indirect costs are allocated more logically – and possibly more fairly – to the extent that final costs and prices will reflect the actual costs used in production. On the other hand, this approach, though precise, can be time-consuming, while in the final analysis some full-cost decisions might be fairly subjective or arbitrary.

Contribution or marginal costing

Contribution costing assumes that direct costs are the same as variable costs and treats fixed costs as indirect costs. This method is straightforward as it simply involves deducting the variable costs from the selling price. The amount which remains is called the 'contribution', as it is the contribution that that particular operational process makes to meeting overheads or fixed costs and profit. An individual business may use target levels of contribution in order to decide on which lines to produce and which to abandon. Alternatively, production may continue as long as the contribution is positive – at least those outputs are making a contribution towards meeting fixed costs and generating a profit.

One advantage of this approach is that it is simple and takes into account the revenue that a particular operation will generate. However, contribution (or marginal) costing may encourage the production of goods or services which, had other costing methods been applied, would have been shown to be loss-making.

Economies and diseconomies of scale

The analysis of costs is borrowed from economic analysis and focuses on the relationship between costs and changes in the size of operations. Put very simply, merely increasing the size of an operation may lead to falls in average or unit costs. These are called **economies of scale**. On the other hand, increasing the size of an operation might lead to falling efficiency and rising average or unit costs. These are referred to as **diseconomies of scale**. The remainder of the chapter looks at these in turn.

Economies of scale

Understanding about the existence and sources of economies of scale goes a long way in helping to explain why small businesses often find it so difficult to compete with larger businesses. For example, most people are conscious of the differences in prices charged by large supermarkets and small local shops. Supermarkets can afford to cut their prices (if they choose to) because they are able to exploit economies of scale. These can be further subdivided into internal and external economies of scale.

Internal economies of scale

These are reductions in unit costs associated directly with the growth in size of the operations unit. They can be classified as technical, organizational, purchasing or financial.

• Technical economies

Larger operational units like out-of-town supermarkets cater for such a high volume of customers that they can afford sophisticated and expensive equipment which contributes to increased efficiency and lower unit costs. Large supermarkets can invest in the quickest and most reliable scanning technologies. The use of their electronic point of sale (EPOS) systems increases the throughput of customers, and provides extensive data on which some other operations management decisions can be speeded up and automated. Thus stock control and reordering can be done virtually automatically, ensuring that the products customers want to buy are (almost) always on the shelves. Moreover, the use of this technology means that large supermarkets can respond both quickly and flexibly to changes in customer requirements.

Small outlets will not have the volume of sales to justify expenditure on expensive yet highly efficient equipment. This means that some operations management functions such as stock control and purchasing have to be completed manually, slowing down these processes and putting up unit costs.

The same principle can be applied to all other organizations almost irrespective of their principal production or service functions. Increasing the scale of operations enables many businesses to move from one-off, to batch, to mass and even, in some cases, to flow production. Each of these different operational processes is associated with potential decreases in unit costs.

• Organizational economies

A large supermarket can afford, for the reasons outlined above, to employ specialist staff, who will bring greater expertise and potentially higher productivity to their particular jobs. These employees range from bakers, to butchers, to shelf stackers, to personnel managers. Large organizations such as Tesco and Sainsburys can afford to employ further specialized staff operating out of headquarters. These centralized functions include marketing, store design, financial control and the like, and all stores in the respective group benefit from this particular economy.

Conversely, a small store will only be able to employ a handful of workers, each will have to undertake a range of tasks and it is unlikely that such workers will be as productive as supermarket specialists.

• Purchasing economies

We are all familiar with the principle of discounts for bulk purchases. Buy more and more of something and the unit price, per gram or kilo for example, is usually reduced. It is in the interests of suppliers to increase the volume of sales by discounting.

Large organizations have an even greater opportunity to cut the cost of their purchases because of the market power they are able to exert. Woolworths, Tesco and Sainsburys, for example, account for over half of the total sales of Cadbury chocolate products in the UK. This gives these large businesses great bargaining power when it comes to negotiating prices with suppliers. The relationship between customer and supplier becomes even more uneven when the latter is relatively small. Farmers have long complained about the unfair buying power exerted by the supermarkets.

Many small retailers attempt to cope with the buying power of their larger competitors by agreeing to exclusive contracts with particular wholesalers. Spar-branded stores are an example of this competitive response.

Councils' plan to cut costs with online buying

DOUG CAMERON

A local government agency will launch an Internet-based purchasing system this summer designed to slice up to £4bn from councils' annual spending.

The Improvement and Development Agency, a policy forum backed by the Local Government Association, will today shortlist two north American-backed consortia to operate its 'ideal marketplace' nationally after a trial involving about 20 councils.

Gary Richardson, the agency's director of business development, said the 409 councils in England and Wales spent some £27.5bn a year on goods and services including £2.5bn on transaction costs.

The platform aims to combine councils' purchasing power and cut costs. It also aims to turn some councils into centres of excellence to co-ordinate national buying.

It will include a matrix allowing councils to balance best-price with other factors such as supporting local suppliers.

Financial Times, 7 February 2001

- *Financial economies*

Crucially, large organizations often have access to cheaper finance than smaller competitors. Most large private-sector businesses in the UK are public limited companies (plcs), and share issues can be a cheaper way of financing expansion than bank loans or alternative sources of finance. In any case, the same purchasing economies apply when large organizations choose to raise capital from the banks and other financial institutions.

Similarly, large organizations have access to international money markets and competitive pressures there tend to reduce interest rates (i.e. the cost of borrowing) still further. From a lender's point of view, large companies are more likely to have substantial assets which can be offered as security for a loan. Few of these opportunities to cut the cost of borrowing are available to small businesses. Often their relationships with banks are less than friendly. From the lender's point of view, loans to small businesses carry more risk – and this is used to justify higher interest charges and the heavier 'policing' of loans.

External economies of scale

These are reductions in unit costs in an organization which occur not directly as a result of its own growth, but as a result of that of the industry as a whole. These economies are most common when the growth of an industry is concentrated in a particular region.

For example, even small firms producing or providing services to the ICT market will benefit if they are close to other businesses in the supply chain. Thus, Swindon, Reading and Cambridge are all areas associated with the development of ICT technologies, creating a larger pool of skilled labour, specialist training by local colleges and access to research and development through local universities. Each of these factors can contribute to lower unit costs than would otherwise be the case.

Diseconomies of scale

The growth of an organization is no *guarantee* of lower unit costs. Diseconomies of scale can be categorized similarly to economies of scale: internal (technical, organizational and marketing) and external.

Internal diseconomies of scale

- *Technical diseconomies*

Continual increases in the volume of output do not always result in continuing reductions in unit costs. Considerable research has been undertaken to investigate the optimum size of an individual plant, and this indicates that in most industries technical diseconomies tend to occur if growth exceeds particular levels.

For example, the cost of transporting oil by sea falls dramatically as bigger bulk carriers are used. There are, however, technical limits to this expansion, and building ships above a particular tonnage is not possible. Similarly, increasing dependence upon a very few plants using mass production techniques can increase the risk of production failing because of the breakdown of some small part or non-supply of a particular component.

• *Organizational diseconomies*
An increase in the volume of operations is often associated with an increase in the sheer size of an organization. However, larger organizations are more difficult to manage efficiently. Communications become more difficult. Bureaucracy and red tape might drive up overheads and hence unit costs, and workers might become less well motivated. If all these factors come into play, a large organization can become inefficient and unresponsive to customers' needs.

These problems are sometimes compounded when large organizations are insulated from competitive pressures because they dominate particular industries. They can use their market power to limit competition, or to take over potential competitors. This kind of activity can decrease operational efficiency and push up unit costs.

The existence of this kind of diseconomy can explain the break-up of some organizations in both the private and public sectors. Thus the demerger of ICI and Zeneca, along with the privatization of British Rail, were both driven by a desire to create leaner, fitter, more competitive organizations able to reduce unit costs.

• *Marketing diseconomies*
As indicated in the previous section, large uncompetitive organizations are more likely to lose their customer focus. They are likely to be less responsive to changes in customers' demands. They are more likely to defend and maintain their existing markets rather than seek new markets. Thus, large organizations might be less innovative, and in the long run this too will contribute to rising unit costs.

External diseconomies off scale
These are especially likely to occur if industries grow rapidly within particular areas which may be locationally inappropriate. Thus, the garment industry in central and eastern London suffers from problems in recruiting staff, difficulties in transportation, and cramped and often

inefficient premises. All these factors associated with the growth of a particular industry in a particular area will contribute to rising unit costs.

KEY WORDS

Break-even analysis	Private cost
Fixed costs	Social cost
Variable costs	Direct costs
Total costs	Indirect costs
Average cost	Full-cost technique
Unit cost	Absorption costing
Marginal cost	Contribution costing
Opportunity cost	Economies of scale
External costs	Diseconomies of scale

Further reading

Barnes, S., *Essential Business Studies*, Collins Educational, 1997.

Grant, S., and Vidler, C., Part 1, Unit 11, in *Economics in Context*, Heinemann Educational, 2000.

Griffiths, A., and Wall, S., *Applied Economics: An Introductory Course*, 8th edn, Longman, 2000.

Izhar, R., *Accounting Costing and Management*, Oxford University Press, 1996.

Useful websites

Bized: www.bized.ac.uk/virtual/cb/factory/production/worksheets5.htm (worksheets on break-even analysis)

Bized: www.bized.ac.uk/virtual/cb/factory/accounts/intro1.htm (on types of costs)

Essay topic

Choose a local business and analyse the make-up of its costs of production. Identify those which could be reduced and indicate how you think this might be best achieved.　　　　　　　[25 marks]

Data response question

This task is based on part of an OCR Business Studies specimen paper issued in 2000. Read the piece that follows before answering the questions.

Smythe plc

Smythe plc is based in the UK and makes shirts. Production capacity is 400 000 units per annum. Sales volume is currently 145 000 per annum. The shirts are sold by Smythe to retailers at a price of £16 each. Table A shows the company's cost structure.

Table A Smythe's cost structure (per unit produced)

Variable costs	
Labour	£3.00
Maintenance	£0.60
Materials	£2.80
Overhead cost per unit (at maximum capacity)	
Total overhead per unit	£2.91

Most economic forecasters expect the pound sterling to decrease in value over the next three years as measured against the euro and most major foreign currencies.

Smythe is considering increasing its production level to maximum capacity and attempting to sell in the lower-priced market segments, possibly under a different brand name, whilst retaining existing sales. Table B shows its analysis of the market.

Table B The UK shirt market by sector

Sales volume	Price to retailer	Importer share of the market	Retailers
175 million	£4–6	80%	Supermarkets, chain stores, mail order
20 million	£8–13	12%	Multiple tailors, independents
5 million	£14–18	3%	Prestigious department stores, other quality outlets

1. Explain the term 'variable costs' as used in Table A. [4 marks]
2. Define and then calculate for Smythe plc:
   (a) the break-even level of output; [6 marks]
   (b) the current margin of safety. [4 marks]
3. Discuss whether Smythe's idea of selling in the lower-priced market segments is likely to be successful. [15 marks]

Chapter Four

Locating operations

Study of locational factors often reveals the significance of historical accident and subjective decision-making. Nonetheless, the whereabouts of production or service functions will have a major influence on the profitability or viability of an organization.

The most fundamental operations management decision concerns the actual location of an organization. Study of locational factors often reveals the significance of historical accident and subjective decision-making. Nonetheless, the whereabouts of production or service functions will have a major influence on the profitability or viability of an organization.

Traditionally, location decisions have often been heavily constrained by limiting factors such as access to markets or materials. However, technological developments have meant that the location of many operations is now much more fluid. This chapter investigates factors which may explain location decisions taken by organizations and considers the significance of the technological factors which now make location decisions far less constrained.

Traditional locational factors

Decisions about location involve reconciliation of the range of conflicting factors whose relative importance will vary according to the particular characteristics of the transformation process. These factors include the following:

- markets
- resources
- transport
- site requirements
- labour supply
- government intervention
- inertia
- the 'X' factor.

Markets

Location decisions have traditionally been strongly affected by the pull acting upon the transformation process by access to markets. This can be modelled using the input–output model outlined in Chapter 1.

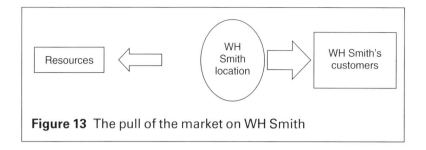

Figure 13 The pull of the market on WH Smith

WH Smith's retail operation consists of selling newspapers, magazines, greeting cards, stationery, music and gaming products. As theirs is a service-based activity their most significant inputs to the transformation are customers, to which must be added stock and staff. They sell large volumes of relatively low-value items, many of which are casual or impulse purchases. They need, therefore, to be as close to their customers as possible. Hence the pull of the market is far greater than the relative pull of other factors, which explains their location on the high streets of towns and cities at (not, it should be added, on the high street of any town, but those large enough to generate particular levels of demand), railway stations and at airports . This is illustrated in Figure 13.

Resources

Oil refining is a highly capital-intensive operation which involves the transformation of crude oil into a variety of products. In this case it pays to locate such operations close to sources of crude oil. Thus most oil refineries in the UK are located at ports or access points close to the various sources of crude oil – Central America, the Middle East, Nigeria and the North Sea. It also pays to transform the crude into a variety of products before final distribution to industrial and retail customers. This is illustrated diagrammatically in Figure 14 and by the map in Figure 15.

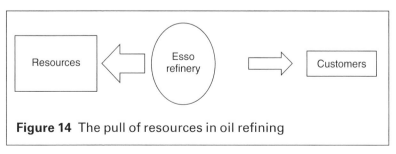

Figure 14 The pull of resources in oil refining

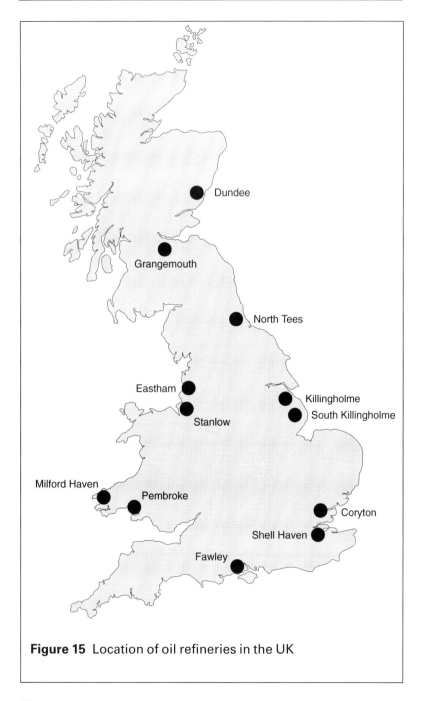

Figure 15 Location of oil refineries in the UK

Another useful way of looking at resources and the transformation process when applied to production is to ask whether the transformation process is bulk-enhancing or -reducing.

For example, the production of beer is bulk-enhancing to the extent that large quantities of water are added to relatively small amounts of hops, sugar and malted barley. Traditionally the high transportation costs of the finished product compared with the low transportation costs of materials other than water would result in breweries being located in towns and near rivers.

Alternatively the production of alumina, the semi-processed raw material used in the production of aluminium, results in the production of large amounts of waste. Hence the transformation process is bulk-reducing and the transport costs of shipping alumina is far less than that of shifting bauxite from its few sources around the world to nearer its eventual market. Alumina production, therefore, is usually located close to sources of bauxite.

Transport

It should be clear that all the factors discussed above are interrelated. Good transport links can in some cases compensate for distance from markets. Improvements and reductions in the cost of air transport have made the transport of low-bulk items relatively cheap and made the acquisition of partly finished goods from around the world more feasible. Over 80 per cent of goods in the UK are transported by road. Examination of the concentration of business activities along the UK's motorway system shows the importance that many companies attach to good road links. Similarly the proximity of ports and airports pulls a range of businesses. Alternatively, distance from quick and reliable transport acts as a powerful *constraint* upon the location of business activity, as economic planners in Cornwall, the north-west of Scotland and western Wales know to their cost.

Site requirements

Different transformation processes have different site requirements. Large production operations need space, and – when planning for the future – they need opportunities for further expansion.

Honda motor company has a great competitive advantage over Rover when the nature of the sites of their respective operations is compared. Honda assembles cars on a large flat 'greenfield' site on the edge of Swindon, surrounded by land available for further development. Rover's plant at Longbridge, in contrast, is cramped in an urban area and at one point a bridge has been built to accommodate a conveyor belt linking two parts of the plant over a major road.

Potential sites of the same size attract different rents, and in those operations in which rent forms a high proportion of costs, businesses are less likely to locate where rents are high.

Labour supply

For organizations in which the labour input is important, either as a proportion of total costs or in terms of particular skills, the supply of labour might be a particularly strong influence on location decisions.

Japanese car manufacturers like Toyota and Nissan have deliberately chosen sites for operations in the UK which offer plentiful supplies of labour and a tradition of manufacturing, but they have chosen not to site plant close to traditional centres of car production. They prefer to train their workforces rather than rely on a supply of skilled motor manufacturing workers, such as would be found in the West Midlands, Merseyside or the East End of London.

Many **transnational companies** in the UK are finding it increasingly difficult to recruit workers with the right level of ICT skills. Some companies cluster where there are already other employers of workers with ICT skills (e.g. Reading and Swindon) because they think they will be able to attract (poach) these workers by offering higher rates of pay. Other companies take the more radical step of locating operations in countries such as India, Malaysia and Singapore, whose governments have made the provision of ICT training a priority.

Where transformation requires large numbers of low-skilled workers, operations are likely to be found in those regions where labour costs are lowest.

Government intervention

Governments have always had a significant effect on location decisions. Various **government incentives** are used to attract inward investment, and hence operations, to particular locations.

The European Union classifies all the regions in member states according to their income and unemployment levels. Regions whose incomes fall below European averages by particular amounts qualify for 'Objective 1' status, which means that grants are available to develop infrastructure and provide training to make such regions more attractive to inward investment. Cornwall is an example of such an area; but whether such incentives are sufficient to outweigh the problems which stem from being so far from, and so poorly connected to, potential markets is an open question.

Governments can also influence tax levels charged to organizations. They use planning laws to limit particular processes to particular locations, and some regions have succeeded in undertaking highly effective public relations campaigns to attract particular types of business. For example, the civic leaders of Bonn responded to the movement of capital status to Berlin by emphasizing the attractiveness of Bonn to e-commerce and related ICT activities.

Not all government intervention is so up-front and obvious. Bribery and corruption is common in many countries. Transnational companies are sometimes able to override objections to particular locations, or minimize local taxation, by offering 'inducements' to government officials. Planning decisions in this country are said by some to involve secret agreements through such shadowy organizations as the Freemasons.

Inertia

Once operations have been located in a particular place, changed market or production factors do not always lead to a change of location. Organizations grow and develop in particular areas, which might have been the most cost-effective location historically. Once established, **inertia** often limits the consideration of alternatives, especially if large amounts of investment are involved; hence the efforts to keep car manufacturers in the Midlands, and at Longbridge in particular. Mention has already been made of the inefficiencies associated with location in a crumbling urban area, but the political consequences of the closure of this factory have helped ensure that production continues in an inappropriate location.

The 'X' factor

No consideration of location can be complete without reference to the strange and unpredictable effects of chance and historical accident that have led to the location of certain operations in particular cities and regions.

The garment industry which still survives in central and east London owes its origins partly to the influx of refugees. Jews from eastern Europe at the turn of the century, and Turks, Greeks and Bangladeshis in more recent years, have helped provide both skills and enterprise to this industry. The birthplace or home of particular inventors or innovators such as Henry Ford provide the 'X' factor to explain the location of particular businesses, and research indicates that the whim or tastes of managing directors can override other locational factors.

Geography and history still matter

JOHN KAY

Geography matters – because even if the distribution of natural resources is no longer of overriding importance, the distribution of man-made resources is. Above all, the distribution of capital drives both personal standards of living and business location. Not just capital in the narrow sense of investment in plant and machinery, but human capital – investment in education – and social capital: the political and legal infrastructure and culture of personal relationships within which business is done. And the distribution of such capital is as uneven as the distribution of natural resources was during the industrial revolution.

Yet the distribution of capital, particularly physical capital, is not set by nature but determined by people. With freedom of capital movement, its owners can locate capital where they will and they do not do so on nationalistic or patriotic grounds. Which is why differences in social capital are crucial. In a globalized world of freely moving capital and increasingly freely moving people, it is only social capital that remains tied to specific locations.

These differences in institutions are the main influence on differences in living standards. And differences in social institutions also explain the localisation of what would otherwise seem to be footloose production. Tacit skills and knowledge are developed where people exchange ideas with each other casually and daily. Flexible production relationships are based on personal relationships.

The information that can be handled by information technology is of a limited kind. Some of the data needed for financial services business can be found on screens. But much of it cannot. It needs not only body language but also the nuances that can be conveyed only between people who are, or have been, in the same room. The chat room is an impoverished form of human interaction and e-mail an impoverished form of human communication.

So geography continues to matter and because geography matters, history matters too. It is not an accident that tie-making is centred in Italy and software production in the US and that financial services are strong in England. These capabilities can be traced back to specific elements in the social and economic histories of the respective countries – the flourishing of design skills in Italy during the Renaissance, the early development of a large installed base of computers in the US, the pivotal role of English merchants in the development of trading economies.

It is an accident that these activities are more specifically located near Lake Como, in Silicon Valley and between Holborn and Aldgate. But such accidents of history are not easily reversed. As the evolution of London investment banking in the last decade has shown, the identity of the participants may change but the location of the activity does not. So long as culture matters, history and geography will matter too.

Financial Times, 10 January 2001

Thus, so-called 'good' schools, exclusive housing, or environmentally attractive areas can all exert a pull on locational decisions.

Scientific or quasi-scientific methods used to aid location decisions

One approach used by organizations is to make a list of those factors identified as possibly influencing location, and to *weigh* each one according to the particular importance to the operations under consideration.

For example, an American candy manufacturer seeking to establish a plant in Europe might identify and assess the relative importance of location factors as shown in Figure 16. The percentage figure in the weighting column is the company's subjective assessment of the importance of each factor.

In this example, the 30 per cent allocated to transport shows that this factor is considered to be twice as important as the impact of government intervention, in this case grants and tax breaks. The Ireland column records the scores given by the operations director for that country against each of the seven criteria in the first column. These figures are multiplied by the appropriate weighting to give a weighted score. Thus Ireland scores 150 under access to markets. This process is repeated for possible Spanish locations, giving a weighted score of 240 for markets. The overall scores for these countries are 490 and 645, with Spain therefore being the preferred location.

This process is **quasi-scientific**. Although it is objective, because it forces the operations director to consider locational factors and to

Location factor	Weighting	Ireland		Spain	
		Score	Weighted	Score	Weighted
Markets	30%	5	150	8	240
Resources	5%	2	40	9	45
Transport	30%	2	60	8	240
Site requirements	10%	7	70	2	20
Labour supply	5%	2	10	6	30
Government intervention	15%	8	120	4	60
PR	5%	8	40	2	10
Total	100%		490		645

Figure 16 A scoring system to determine best location

assess their relative importance, the assessments for each country against each criterion can only be described as subjective. Hence the term 'quasi-' or 'almost-' scientific is appropriate. Nonetheless, it is probably better for the business to use such techniques than rely on the prejudices and personal demands of the managing director.

Globalization and the loosening of location decisions

A number of factors have contributed to what has been described as the **globalization** of operations decisions. These include:

- reductions in the relative cost of transport
- increasing reliability of transport systems
- improvements in communications technology
- an increase in size and number of transnational organizations.

None of these factors is necessarily more important than any other. Each interacts with the others, and when added together they have resulted in globalization which has had fundamental effects on both operations management decisions and on whole economies and societies.

• Transport costs

Containerization of sea transport has cut the costs and delivery times of goods transported by sea. Comparable improvements in air freight have meant that transport costs for many non-bulky products are now a relatively small proportion of the final costs of many goods. For example, Next can afford to air-freight most of the clothes that it sells in the UK from suppliers in Hong Kong, China and other parts of the Far East.

• Transport reliability

The factors identified above have combined with improvements in reliability to ensure that, if required, most products can be delivered from and to most parts of the world within 36 hours. Similarly, sea transport has become more reliable, with regular scheduled services linking major production centres with their markets.

• Communications

Computer technology has revolutionized communications. Telephone, e-mail, fax and video-conferencing all provide instant access not just to ideas and people but also to complicated systems associated with production. It is possible for a designer sitting in front of a computer in Bristol to communicate in real time with a printing facility in Singapore. Goods can be designed here and made there.

• Transnational corporations

More and more operations management decisions are taken by transnational corporations. The size and power of these organizations is enormous. The annual turnover of companies such as Exxon, Unilever, General Motors and Nestlé exceeds the national income of many of the world's states.

These organizations operate and market their outputs in many locations around the world. Although no common strategy is followed, all use their immense economic power in ways that have a significant effect on people worldwide. The growth in importance of transnational corporations increases globalization in a number of ways. Some, like Honda, argue that if they are to achieve long-term profits from global sales they should locate different operations in different parts of the world. Building a plant in Swindon was the outcome of a marketing strategy that aimed at ensuring that Honda was seen to be investing significantly in one of their important markets. Other transnational corporations encourage competition between what are seen as rival plants in different locations.

The growth of transnationals also increases the speed at which technology, or the ways in which things are made, can be transferred from one location to another.

Finally, companies such as Microsoft, Coca-Cola and Benetton are anxious to build universally attractive global images for their products. In short, many businesses now produce products and services that are sourced globally for global markets.

Globalization of locational decisions

The combined impact of the above factors is that:

- cost differences between different global operations locations are reduced
- the particular advantages of certain locations are reduced
- many operations become 'footloose', meaning that operations can be quickly switched from one country to another.

```
┌─────────────────────────────────────────────────────┐
│                     KEY WORDS                         │
│                                                       │
│   The 'X' factor              Greenfield              │
│   Quasi-scientific            Transnational companies │
│   Globalization               Government incentives   │
└─────────────────────────────────────────────────────┘
```

Further reading

Micklethwait, J., *Future Perfect*, Heinemann, 2000.

Schmenner, R., *Making Business Location Decisions*, Prentice Hall, 1982.

Tinniswood, P., *Marketing and Production Decisions*, Longman, 1991.

Useful websites

Bized: www.bized.ac.uk/stafsup/options/location.htm (practical worksheets on location decisions)

Bized: www.bized.ac.uk/compfact/bp/bpindex.htm (indicates location of a transnational corporation)

Oneworld.net and Corporate Watch: www.oneworld.org and www.corporatewatch.org.uk (critical view of transnationals)

Essay topic

Xerox is currently restructuring its global production strategy and is planning to cut production in the UK and Holland, as well as increase output in China, Mexico and eastern Europe. Assess the likely impact of these changes on the future performance of this corporation.

[25 marks]

Data response question

This task is based on part of an OCR Business Studies specimen paper issued in 2000. Read the piece below (adapted from the *Sunday Times* of 22 August 1999) before answering the questions.

Ford moves European HQ out of Britain

Ford has moved the headquarters of its European operations from Britain to Germany. The shift is intended to increase the American group's competitiveness in the continent's biggest single market, Germany. The move will be seen as a blow to the prestige of British industry. Ford of Europe has been based in Warley, Essex, not far from Ford's Dagenham plant, since Henry Ford II, grandson of the company's founder, set up the European organization in 1967. Ford of Europe is now based at Cologne, Germany.

The shift may arouse fears about Ford's commitment to Britain. Its Welsh engine factory in Bridgend is at present competing with Germany and Spanish plants to win a project for which Ford are seeking about £60m in aid from the British government. There have also been intermittent concerns about whether Ford would maintain its dual-site engineering operation in Europe, under which design and engineering is divided between Cologne and Essex. However, the company has invested heavily in its Essex facility in recent years. As evidence that there is no intention of pulling back further, Ford can point to its decision to expand the production line at Dagenham, the lead plant in Europe for production of its Fiesta car. In addition, Ford's newly created Premier Auto Group, which is made up of Jaguar, Aston Martin, Volvo and Lincoln, is based in Britain.

Ford of Britain has also been the test-bed for Ford's efforts to establish itself as the world's leading supplier of automotive services as well as vehicles. In April, Ford surprised the European car industry when it paid £1b for Kwik-Fit, the vehicle-repair chain. It is also expanding into car retailing and financial services in Britain. Ford has successfully resisted challenges to its position of market supremacy, and it has more than 18% share of the UK car market. But Ford is struggling in Germany where its market share, excluding Jaguar, has slipped below 9% this year. As a result, its European share has skidded well below the 12% at which it stood two years ago.

Ford managers believe that only by rooting itself in Germany can Ford of Europe avoid being handicapped in its attempts to match its American arch-rival, General Motors, and the European market leader, Volkswagen. Success in Germany is crucial to Ford's attempts to improve sluggish profitability. Germany is almost twice the size of the next-largest European markets – Italy, Britain and France – and accounts for about one-quarter of total west European car sales. General Motors has established a European lead over Ford thanks largely to its presence in Germany, where its Opel brand is seen as German whereas Ford is seen as a foreign brand.

1. The article suggests that one reason why Ford has moved its European headquarters to Germany is 'to improve sluggish profitability'. Outline *two* other possible objectives Ford may have been pursuing when deciding to move its European HQ to Germany. [4 marks]

2. By considering the determinants of demand, outline why the German market is 'almost twice the size' of Britain's. [10 marks]

3. Discuss the objectives the British government may have in giving Ford financial aid for its Welsh engine plant. [15 marks]

Chapter Five

Planning and controlling operations

The most important function of the operations manager is to ensure that the inputs of the transformation process are married up with, or reconciled to, the outputs of that process. Failure to do so will bring the transformation to a halt.

Planning and controlling operations refers to all those activities linked to the **transformation process**. The most important function of the operations manager is to ensure that the inputs of the transformation process are married up with, or reconciled to, the outputs of that process. Failure to do so will bring the transformation to a halt. It follows from the analysis in Chapter 1 that the nature of the transformation process itself will have a significant effect on the planning and control of operations, and this chapter provides an introduction to understanding how these processes might be managed. Consideration is given to:

- the nature of planning and control
- the effect of the type of transformation process on planning and control
- different activities associated with planning and control.

Finally, the significance of aggregate planning and control is considered. This involves decisions about the overall capacity of an organization to ensure that consumers' demands are met, ensuring both high levels of customer satisfaction and – depending on the objectives of the organization – a high level of profit or a satisfactory surplus.

The nature of planning and control

Planning and control are those functions which ensure that outputs are met by ensuring that inputs are available:

- in the right amounts
- at the right time
- at an acceptable level of quality.

Only if these objectives are met will the organization have the capability of meeting customer **demand**.

For example, GlaxoSmithKline (GSK) produce Lucozade, Ribena

and a range of other drinks at a factory in Gloucestershire. A key element in the company's operations is called 'the dispensary'. This is where all the ingredients making up particular drinks are measured and prepared for inclusion on one of the production lines. Failure to include the correct amount of flavouring in a particular batch would result in the loss of, say, 150 000 cans of Lucozade. Similarly, wrongly timed or sequenced batches will halt production, and the inclusion of ingredients of an unacceptable quality might carry health risks – which would threaten the continued existence of the factory and its owners.

Planning refers to those operations which involve anticipating and preparing for the future. In the case of GSK, this will involve deciding upon which products are needed most quickly and which can wait. It also involves the sequencing of activities as the same production lines are used to produce a range of variants on the basic products – Lucozade and Ribena. Planning also includes decision-making about when production lines need replacing or upgrading, which will tend to be done at those times of the year when demand is not at its peak.

Control relates to the checks and balances which are put into operation when production actually starts. The ingredients are literally mixed together and the timing of the addition of one element, such as sugar, is regulated by a programmed machine. Checks take place all down the line to ensure that strict quality standards are met.

Managing inputs and outputs

The characteristics of the demand for different products and services will vary. The demand for certain products such as bread and milk is fairly stable and predictable. This makes operations management decisions about planning and control easier. Outputs can be closely tailored to meet anticipated changes in demand, **buffer stocks** will be minimized and the inputs can be planned and managed to meet **production targets**.

When demand is less predictable, the planning and control functions have to be managed differently. Running all but the most popular restaurants is usually nerve-racking for the owners or managers. The demand for this kind of service is notoriously difficult to predict, although it might be possible to discern broad annual trends, with peaks of demand in the summer and the run-up to Christmas. On a weekly basis, and depending on the location, a weekend will be busier than the early part of the week.

But the restaurant trade is very competitive, and customers can be very fickle. This unpredictable demand will encourage the restaurateur to carry buffer stocks at different stages of the production cycle. Freezers and cold stores need to contain enough ingredients to cope with the busiest of days. The easiest strategy is to carry large stocks of frozen pre-cooked meals, but the attraction of this approach has to be weighed against possible negative reactions from customers, especially if they are paying a lot for their night out. Similar considerations will apply to staffing levels. Unpredicted fluctuations in demand can lead to long waiting times at one extreme, to unemployed staff at the other.

There are three broad strategies which can be followed to match inputs to outputs effectively:

- **resourcing to order**

- **making to stock**

- **making to order.**

Resourcing to order

When a single order places a significant demand on the total resources of an organization – for example a shipyard building a supertanker, a small builder erecting a complete house or a dressmaker creating a wedding dress – it is likely that the arrival of the order will in turn trigger the ordering of the necessary resources. This minimizes the need for buffer stocks and minimizes potential negative cash flow, which can arise if the organization has to wait a long time for sales revenue but still has to pay out for the costs of its inputs. Using this strategy will lead to customers waiting for a minimum of the whole of the production or 'throughput' time.

Making to stock

If each individual output represents a small proportion of the total output of a business, and if the business in question is confident of a continuing but fluctuating demand for its product(s), then operations are likely to be organized on a making-to-stock basis. In this context, operations are managed to maintain a relatively constant throughput, and some output will then be held in stock at each stage in the distribution process.

For example, Cadbury will organize its production runs of particular products and store some or part of the outputs. In this way, buffer stocks can be used to absorb unpredicted changes in demand, and to enable the company to undertake longer production runs, avoiding the down time associated with changing outputs from one product to the next. If making to stock is adopted, delivery times can be very short.

Making to order

Many businesses combine the financial benefits of resourcing to order with the greater stability and orderliness associated with making to stock, by instead making to order.

Today, most car manufacturers plan ahead in terms of daily, weekly and monthly production targets, and order resources accordingly. However, actual customer orders will stimulate the release of appropriate components and the scheduling of production of one particular car, with a particular specification, in direct response to that demand. Thus, a customer requiring a metallic blue, seven-seat diesel Ford Galaxy with air conditioning will trigger the production of a car which meets these requirements, thus minimizing the holding of large buffer stocks containing the particular range of options which customers might require.

This production strategy is likely to result in delivery times which will not be on demand but will be shorter than the 'throughput' time.

The activities associated with planning and control

Businesses whose transformation processes involve producing a range of outputs using similar resources are faced with decisions about when and how much to produce in each production run. This involves consideration of three related yet distinct activities.

- **Loading** refers to decisions about the volume of output which can be attempted. This, if related to a body panel press, would involve working out the proportion of time in a given period which could be allocated to the production of particular body parts. Loading has to take into account non-productive or 'down' time when maintenance takes place, and changeover time between different production runs.

- **Sequencing** involves deciding on the order in which various tasks should be undertaken. A particular criterion or set of criteria is usually used. Thus, customers might get more favourable treatment. Alternatively, prioritization can be made according to the date of promised delivery. Approaches which pay more regard to using productive resources most efficiently may involve sequencing according to the length of time a particular production process takes.

- **Scheduling** involves a set of more detailed decisions as to when one job might start and another finish. **Gantt charts** can be used to illustrate the complexity and change of efficient scheduling. In the example in Figure 17, the horizontal bars represent the time devoted to the completion of the various processes associated with building a house. The Gantt chart can be used to both plan and control the production process. Once prepared it enables the builder to ensure that each stage is timed so that it is completed prior to the work which follows. So plumbing precedes plastering, and foundations follow ground work.

Another decision related to scheduling is whether or not work is pushed or pulled through the various production stages. If **push scheduling** is used, each work centre produces outputs without regard to whether the succeeding work centre can make use of it. Alternatively, **pull scheduling** involves each work centre ordering inputs from previous work centres as and when required. This approach makes a business much more sensitive to customers's requirements and changes in demand. Ultimately, it is the customers who trigger production at each stage. If push scheduling is used, then any slowdown or delay in the production process will result in the build-up of inventory or stocks before the 'bottleneck', and shortages afterwards. The pull approach ensures that only what is needed is produced, so stocks and inventory are less likely to build up.

Aggregate planning and control

Consideration also needs to be given to decisions relating to the overall capacity of an organization to meet customers' demands. Getting such decisions right is likely to be fundamental to the success or otherwise of

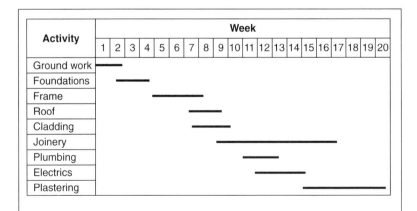

Figure 17 A Gantt chart used to schedule the building of a house

any organization. Planning and investing in over-capacity is a recipe for financial disaster. At the other extreme, failing to plan and invest in sufficient capacity to meet demands will result in unsatisfied and dissatisfied customers – a different but equally threatening route to financial disaster. Therefore it is important for all organizations to pay particular attention to forecasting:

- likely patterns of future demand
- the extent of available capacity.

Fluctuations in demand

Demand forecasting is one of the most important aspects of the marketing function within a business, and it is vital that those responsible for operations management be fully and reliably informed of likely fluctuations in demand. For example, seasonal factors will affect the demand for most goods and services. This quite obviously applies to the effect of Christmas on the sales of retailers, but it also operates in most sectors of the economy. Figure 18 illustrates monthly variations in sales for a branch of a high street retailer like WH Smith.

Such a graph can provide a basis for forecasting future sales patterns and ensuring that production capacity is sufficient to meet expected demand. The crucial capacity factors for WH Smith will be space both

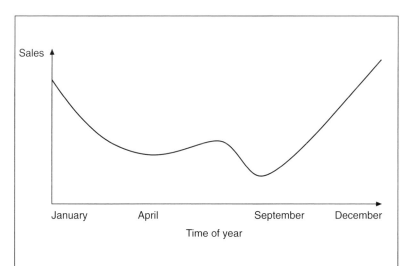

Figure 18 Seasonal variation in sales figures for a typical high street retailer

to store and to display goods, and adequate numbers of staff, both part-time and full-time. Changing capacity in terms of store size is rather difficult and is likely to be part of the company's longer-term strategy.

Compared with WH Smith, companies operating in some sectors have great problems in trying to forecast likely patterns of demand. Predicting sales of meat-based products, new houses and newly formed bands are all fraught with difficulties. Even supermarkets find it hard to predict week-to-week fluctuations for particular branded goods.

Capacity measurement

On the surface this would appear to be an easier task than forecasting demand, as **capacity measurement** involves factors over which an organization has much more direct control.

For example, GSK (mentioned at the beginning of this chapter) can produce 10 000 two-litre bottles of Ribena per eight-hour shift. However, their capacity measurement is more complex than this simple measure would suggest. GSK produces a wide range of variations on basic products like Ribena – outputs aimed at different foreign markets, as well as a growing variety of flavourings and sugar levels. Changeovers between these alternative product lines are likely to reduce actual levels of output from the optimum level.

Another difficulty is that even highly automated systems are unlikely to be able to run flat out for 24 hours a day, 7 days a week, 365 days a year. The design capacity of a plant will measure the maximum output envisaged in the planning stage. The effective capacity will involve making allowances for maintenance, changeovers etc., and the actual output is likely to be even less once allowances have been made for breakdowns, staffing problems and the thousand and one other things that can limit output. These three measures are illustrated graphically in Figure 19.

A related way of measuring capacity is to use the data in Figure 19 in two ratios. Thus:

$$\frac{\text{Actual output}}{\text{Design capacity}} \text{ is called } utilization$$

$$\frac{\text{Actual output}}{\text{Effective capacity}} \text{ is called } efficiency.$$

Both these measures are important in helping businesses to develop strategies to become more effective.

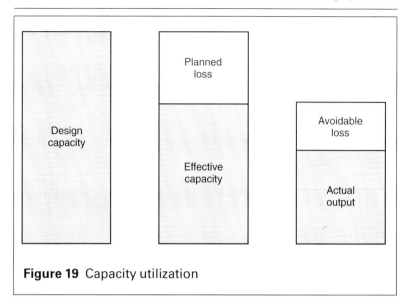

Figure 19 Capacity utilization

Capacity management

There are three theoretical options open to an organization in deciding how to manage capacity in relationship to fluctuations in demand. They can ignore demand, follow demand, or manage demand.

Ignoring demand

This strategy involves producing the same level of output irrespective of variations in demand. For example, Figure 20 illustrates possible levels of demand for greetings cards throughout the year. In months such as May through to November, demand is less than output. Greetings cards produced then will be put into store and released to help cope with the Christmas rush. This strategy allows stable production runs, high utilization ratios and steady employment patterns, and is probably feasible for greetings card production as, relative to their value, cards cost little to store.

This strategy would be wasteful in more labour-intensive transformations as workers would continue to be employed and paid irrespective of the demand for their services. Particular care would have to be taken so that times of excess demand were equally balanced against those periods when inventories were growing.

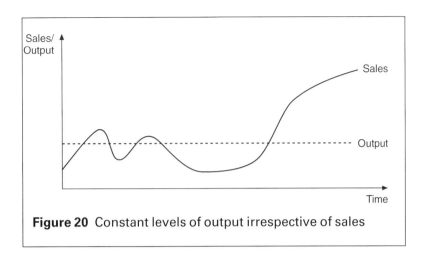

Figure 20 Constant levels of output irrespective of sales

Following demand

As the name implies, this strategy is one in which capacity is varied to meet anticipated fluctuations in demand as far as possible, as shown in Figure 21. This is likely to require regular changes in the inputs of resources, some of which – like skilled labour – might be difficult to switch on and off over short periods. This approach will save on those costs associated with holding stocks, but it carries the danger of not being able to meet unexpected surges in demand.

In spite of the drawbacks, the extremely competitive market conditions faced by many retailers force them to try to tailor capacity

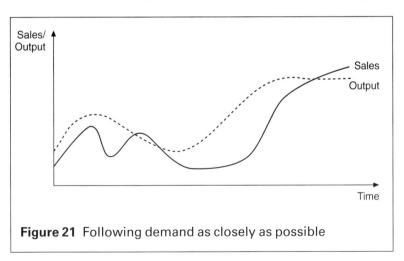

Figure 21 Following demand as closely as possible

as closely as possible to demand. Hence, Tesco used to claim that it will open another checkout if there is a queue of more than two people, and businesses such as McDonald's employ large numbers of young people on very flexible part-time contracts to help match capacity to demand.

Another strategy used with full-time workers is to devise contracts not in terms of daily or weekly hours but for a whole year. These annualized contracts usually involve management giving workers longer holidays, but requiring greater flexibility in terms of the hours worked each day or week.

Managing demand

This is the most challenging and yet potentially the most successful strategy. It aims to combine the benefits of maintaining stable capacity levels with the adverse cost of building up and running large inventories. Managing demand involves evening out the peaks and troughs of demand, as illustrated in Figure 22.

Retailers pursue agile marketing strategies in order to extend particular seasons – leading to the claim that Christmas and Easter come earlier with each passing year. Other festive events such as Mothering Sunday and Father's Day are now heavily promoted as times of card and gift buying.

'Sales' and 'discounts', too, are used to stimulate out-of-season buying. This is a common policy of package tour operators, who may charge double or even treble the price of holidays in popular destinations during school breaks, compared with the remainder of the year.

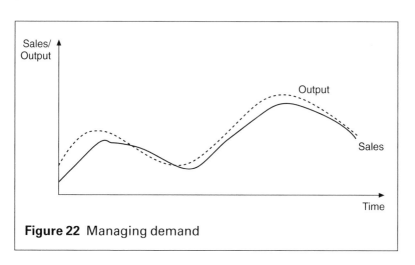

Figure 22 Managing demand

Capacity management in practice

Most organizations are likely to develop **capacity management** strategies that involve a mixture of all three of the approaches outlined above. Thus, there are clear advantages in being able to enjoy steady and constant levels of capacity utilization, and there are usually benefits in building up at least some levels of stock.

At the same time, organizations can be strongly committed to training and recruitment programmes that develop multi-tasking skills which allow labour to be used as flexibly as possible – thereby increasing or decreasing capacity in response to fluctuations in demand.

Finally, marketing departments will aim to develop a range of strategies and product developments in an attempt to even out the impact on capacity utilization of seasonal and other variations in demand.

KEY WORDS

Transformation process	Sequencing
Demand	Scheduling
Buffer stocks	Gantt chart
Production targets	Push scheduling
Resourcing to order	Pull scheduling
Making to stock	Demand forecasting
Making to order	Capacity management
Loading	

Further reading

Galloway, R., *Principles of Operations Management*, Routledge, 1993.

Hill, T., *The Essence of Operations Management*, Prentice Hall, 1993.

Hill, T., *Production/Operations Management*, Prentice Hall, 1995.

Townley, P., *Production*, Longman, 1986.

Useful websites

International Journal of Operations & Production Management: www.mcb.co.uk/ijopm.htm (includes many articles on planning and control)

IndustryWeek: www.industryweek.com (for current issues relating to capacity management)

Essay topic

Choose a local business faced with seasonal variations in demand. Explain why these occur and assess their impact on the functions of the business. Suggest strategies to reduce the adverse effects of the variations you identify. [25 marks]

Data response question

This task is based on an Edexcel sample paper issued in 2000. Imagine that a building contractor has prepared a Gantt chart, as shown below, to identify ways of making effective use of subcontractors and other outside firms in the construction and finishing of two new houses. Study the chart and then answer the question.

Job	Week											
	1	2	3	4	5	6	7	8	9	10	11	12
Clear site	×											
Foundations		×	×									
Lay drains and power cables			×	×								
Erect buildings				×	×	×	×	×	×			
Paint exterior woodwork								×	×	×		
Install electrics and plumbing						×	×					
Decorate exteriors								×	×			
Landscape gardens									×	×		
Remove unwanted materials												×

1. Evaluate the issues which this Gantt chart raises for the firm, with particular reference to the effective use of subcontractors.
[18 marks]

Chapter Six

Project management

... making the Millennium Dome a success, ensuring railways in the UK are safe and mounting a general election campaign are all projects whose complexity is such that failure could ensue if one small detail or operation is overlooked.

This chapter is devoted to an exploration of strategies that can be used to plan and control projects. A project can be defined as a particular set of operations which has a beginning, a middle and an end. The last will involve reaching a predetermined goal by the use of a defined set of resources.

Our working lives are filled with the undertaking of a whole series of projects, some big and some small. Many of these, such as making sure that we get to work or college on time, can be undertaken with very little planning. Similarly in business, we undertake what are in effect a series of semi-automated routines – checking e-mails, opening the post and putting the kettle on.

Project planning, however, is usually associated with unique, larger-scale and more complex operations. Thus, making the Millennium Dome a success, ensuring railways in the UK are safe, and mounting a general election campaign are all projects whose complexity is such that failure could ensue if one small detail or operation is overlooked.

Business theorists and analysts have developed techniques for modelling complex projects, which can be used to both plan and control operations. This chapter considers:

- the **project environment** in which planning and control take place
- **project definition**
- project planning and control, including the use of network or **critical-path analysis.**

The project environment

Projects are different from other kinds of operation. As indicated earlier, they are likely to be a complex set of activities which needs to be managed and controlled to meet a particular objective. Projects are unique in that, strictly defined, they are one-offs. For that reason, uncertainties and the risk of failure are greater.

It follows that the first stage of developing an effective project management system, or framework, involves a rigorous assessment of the environment in which a project will occur.

To take an example, some of the factors that will affect the success or otherwise of the project to increase the safety and reliability of the UK rail network are identified in Figure 23. Identifying and understanding the importance of each of these factors will be crucial to Railtrack. If a key element of the environment is ignored (for example the capacity of subcontractors to supply new line at an acceptable price) then, irrespective of the sophistication of the modelling of the project, it is likely to fail.

Similarly, these factors will contain the uncertainties which collectively affect the successful completion of the project. For instance, the government is a key stakeholder in this process, and the timing of a general election, and increased sensitivity of the government to suggestions of the failure of its transport policies add further uncertainty to the project.

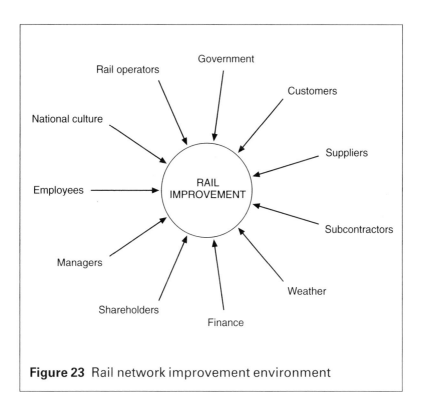

Figure 23 Rail network improvement environment

Project definition

Once the project environment has been carefully mapped it is important to define a project in terms of its **objectives, scope** and **strategy**. These three factors are interrelated and overlap, but each requires careful, thoughtful and imaginative planning to ensure the success of a project.

Defining project *objectives* is both crucial and difficult as this involves anticipating outcomes and deciding on what basis the project is to be judged. There was considerable debate as to how the UK should mark the transition from 1999 to 2000. This started in the early 1990s, when different regions bid for the right to host 'headlining' events. This involved extensive lobbying of the then Conservative government, which finally agreed to the Dome project. Politicians from both major parties wanted an impressive success and decided that the key objective of the Dome was that it should attract 12 million visitors in the year of its operation. Hindsight indicates that this was both an unrealistic and over-optimistic objective. Nonetheless, its existence helped clarify what the project was about and what all those involved had to do to attempt to ensure its success.

Once the overall objective had been set, it was possible to decide and define a series of objectives for each component part or process of the project, and in turn objectives for each subset of these. Thus, accommodating 12 million visitors a year would generate the need to cope with up to 50 000 visitors per day, leading to objectives for sales teams, caterers, cash-handling facilities and the like.

Deciding upon the *scope* of a project involves making clear decisions about what a project can and cannot do; and, similarly, defining boundaries for each of the component parts of a project. Being clear in terms of responsibilities and obligations is vitally important in the effective management of subcontractors.

One of the criticisms of the management of the Dome was that insufficient control was taken over the operations of subcontractors, who, it is alleged, were able to invoice and receive payment for work that had not been clearly agreed at the outset. Greater clarity in defining the scope of the project might have reduced the unanticipated and unplanned outcomes which pushed up the final costs of the project.

Defining a project *strategy* involves deciding how the defined scope and objectives of the project are to be met. This will usually involve breaking down the project into a series of manageable phases or time periods for the completion of particular activities. This allows the setting of 'milestones' or time slots within the life of a project, at which progress can be reviewed. Checks can then be made to ensure that the project is on schedule and whether objectives in terms of costs and quality are being met.

Project planning

Project planning covers a number of key activities, which crucially include determining the cost and timing of a project. Identifying these two key variables, and subjecting them to vigorous analysis, will help determine whether or not a project should start. In the case of the Dome it appears that the decision to go ahead was taken before the initial project-planning phase had been completed. It is often hard to stop a project at this stage.

Project planning also involves identifying the level of resources that will be needed, and this will feed into decisions as to what work is undertaken and how progress is to be monitored. These processes should be repeated during a project, enabling modifications and changes to be made in order to ensure that objectives are met. In the case of the Dome, these reviews usually revealed divergence between project income and costs, requiring additional financial inputs.

A sample project

Key elements in the process of project planning can be shown in relation to organizing a relatively simple event – post-examination celebrations or Summer Balls. This section examines such a 'project'.

- *Purpose:* to celebrate completion of final examinations.
- *Desirable end-result:* majority of year group enjoy themselves.
- *Success criteria:* maximum enjoyment and minimum disturbance of end-of-year celebrations; break-even; health and safety requirements met.
- *Scope:* only final-year students to be invited; prom starts at 9pm and ends at 2am; managed by students; security, catering and music subcontracted.

Stages of the project

1 Clarify details of the event
2 Agree responsibilities
3 Negotiate permissions
4 Agree date and book a venue
5 Book the music
6 Plan promotion and publicity
7 Sell tickets
8 Organize catering and security
9 Prepare the venue
10 Stage the event
11 Clear up
12 Finalize the accounts

Estimate time and resources

The tasks identified above have been placed in a rough order of what needs to be done. Further consideration will need to be given as to how long each activity will take and the level of resources (people) needed to carry it out. Thus, the time taken to complete the first activity – clarifying the details of the event – will depend upon the level for consultation considered appropriate. If all decisions are to be delegated to a small committee, this could be accomplished quite quickly. If on the other hand, extensive consultation with students, staff and even parents is required, more time and resources will have to be allocated.

Scheduling

The **scheduling** stage involves identifying which activities have to be completed before others can be started, and which activities can take place while others are continuing. Sorting out the timing, venue and entertainment must all be done before the publicity can begin. Ticket sales can take place prior to final decisions about security and catering.

This set of relationships is illustrated in Figure 24, which is the Gantt chart we met in Chapter 5. This more sophisticated development of the Gantt can be used to monitor actual progress.

Critical-path analysis

Critical-path analysis (CPA) represents a further development of the use of Gantt charts. As its name implies, it is a modelling exercise which helps identify the most time-effective way of sequencing project activities. CPA also enables the user to predict the effects of delays and changes in project activities.

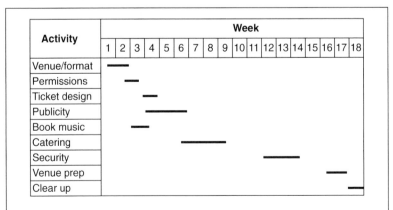

Figure 24 Summer Ball project plan – the Gantt chart

Critical-path networks involve a particular representation of activities. This is illustrated in Figure 25, in which networks of increasing complexity are built up. In each, the straight lines represent particular activities, and the numbers indicate the time units allocated to these activities. The points of transition from one activity to the next are represented by circles, which are known as **nodes**.

In Figure 25(a) there are just two separate activities, relating to the Summer Balls example: designing and printing tickets. A is the design stage and 2 days have been allocated to that task. B is the printing stage, which could take up to 7 days. Printing obviously cannot take place prior to design. Note that, although the length of each stage is clearly indicated, network analysis diagrams do not have to be drawn to scale – in that respect they are a bit like the familiar map of the London Underground.

In Figure 25(b), printing off and displaying posters has been added to the former two-stage process, making a four-stage process. The organizers have decided to mount an initial publicity campaign before the tickets go on sale. Posters can be produced in-house in 2 days as represented by stage C, and it is hoped that their display for 8 days will help boost sales. In this case the poster campaign needs to last for at least 4 days and is represented by stage D. The production and display of posters can go on at the same time as tickets are being printed.

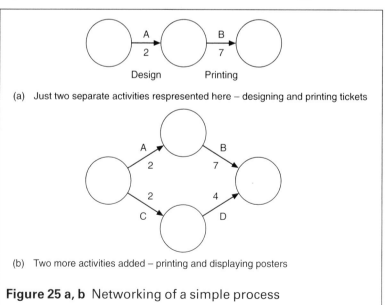

(a)   Just two separate activities respresented here – designing and printing tickets

(b)   Two more activities added – printing and displaying posters

Figure 25 a, b Networking of a simple process

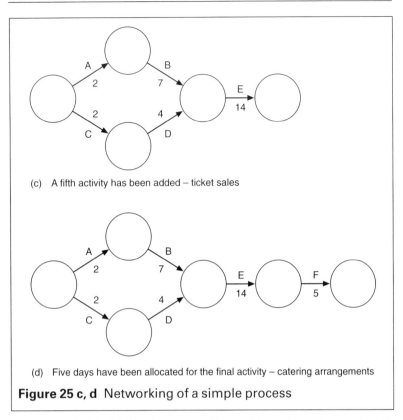

(c)　A fifth activity has been added – ticket sales

(d)　Five days have been allocated for the final activity – catering arrangements

Figure 25 c, d Networking of a simple process

In Figure 25(c), 14 days have been allocated for ticket sales – activity E. This cannot take place before the tickets have been designed and printed.

Figure 25(d) shows the addition of another process, F, as organizers plan to spend 5 days sorting catering arrangements. This involves inviting outside caterers to quote on the basis of ticket sales made at stage E. This simple network can now be used to calculate the length of time taken from the design of tickets until the finalization of catering arrangements by including more information in the nodes representing the transition between one activity and the next (see Figure 26). The left-hand semicircle

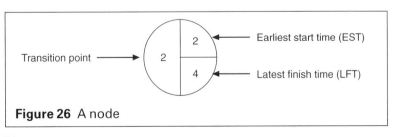

Figure 26 A node

is used to identify the transition point, and the top right quadrant is used to indicate the earliest start time (**EST**) for the next stage – in other words, *the cumulative time taken for all activities up to that point.*

In Figure 27(a), the more detailed nodes have been added to the earlier simplified network. Starting from (1), to get to the point at which tickets will be available for sale at (3) will involve 2 days' design time and 7 days' printing – giving a total of 9 days (spot the entry EST = 9 in one of the nodes). A further 14 days are allocated for ticket sales, giving an EST of 23 days for making catering arrangements, for which a further 5 days are given. This means that the *minimum* time for the completion of this phase of the project plan is 28 days.

Finally, the latest finish time (**LFT**) is indicated by working *backwards* from the end of the project, and deducting the times allocated for each preceding stage. Thus, the LFT for the fifth node would be 28 days less 5 days for stage F. Stages D and B have to be completed before E, giving an LFT for the second node of 2 days. whereas the LFT for the fourth node is 15.

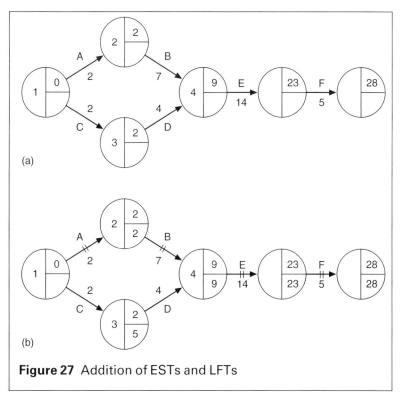

Figure 27 Addition of ESTs and LFTs

Calculating both the latest and earliest finish times provides a means by which the **critical path** can be illustrated. This will be shown by joining all those nodes with the same ESTs and LFTs. This is called the critical path because if there were any hold-ups at any stage along this path the project would be delayed. The path is indicated by two lines on each of the critical activities, as in Figure 27(b).

In this simple example, the design and printing of tickets is crucial. Extra time spent on these activities will add days to the time needed to complete the whole project. However, the organizers can be a bit more relaxed about the design and display of posters. The third node indicates that the latest finish time for the production of posters is 5 days, yet the earliest planned time for completing that process is only 2 days. More time and/or fewer resources could be allocated to this task without affecting the overall timing of the completion of the project. This spare time of 3 days is known as **float time**.

Further network development
There is often a need for more complicated networks than that shown in Figure 27. For example, Figure 28(a) illustrates the development of a network involving 12 separate activities.

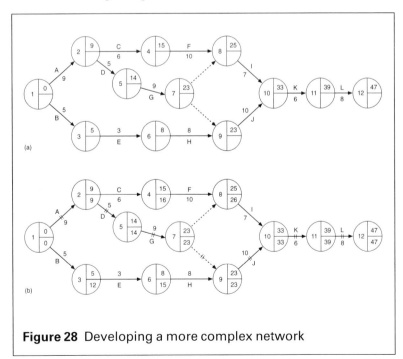

Figure 28 Developing a more complex network

As in the earlier example, activities B, E and H can be carried out at the same time as A, C, F, D and G. Similarly, activities K and L require the completion of all previous activities. The dotted lines between G and I and J indicate 'dummy' activities. These are used in network analysis to indicate that particular activities have to be completed prior to others, but that no time or resources are taken up. Hence there is no number of days associated with the dotted lines.

Note that the ESTs are always calculated as the longest time to reach a particular activity. Thus the EST for activity I is 25 days. There are two routes which could be followed prior to I; they are A–C–F which would take 25 days, or A–D–G which would take 23 days. The longest path must be chosen. Hence the EST for I is 25.

This network is further developed in Figure 28(b) by adding LFTs – again working backwards from the end of the project. Note that the same rules apply – where there are two routes backwards to an activity the *shortest* route is used to calculate the LFTs. Thus working back from C to A gives an LFT of 16 – 6 = 10; however, D to A gives an LFT of 14 – 5 = 9. The lower of these two values becomes the LFT for A.

Calculating all the LFTs allows the critical path to be drawn. This links the nodes containing the same LFTs and ESTs, showing the links between activities which must be made if the project is to be completed in the minimum possible time. Any delays along this path will slow up the whole project. The non-critical path(s) will contain float time. This can take two forms: **free float** and **total float**. These are calculated for any activity by using the following formulas:

Total float = LFT of activity – duration – EST of activity

Free float = EST of following activity – duration – EST of activity.

The calculations of these two kinds of float are illustrated by concentrating on activity E, as shown in Figure 29. In this example the *total float* is 15 – 3 – 5 = 7 days. This means that activity E can be delayed for up to 7 days without slowing down the project as a whole. However, the *free float* calculation for E is 8 – 3 – 5 = 0 days, which means that any delay in activity E will delay the start of activity H.

The total and free floats can also be calculated for activity H, as shown in Figure 30. Here the *total* float calculation is 23 – 8 – 8 = 7 days, while the *free float* also works out to be 23 – 8 – 8 = 7 days. In this case a delay of up to 7 days would not hold up either the whole project or the next activity.

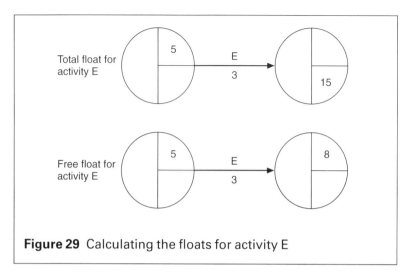

Figure 29 Calculating the floats for activity E

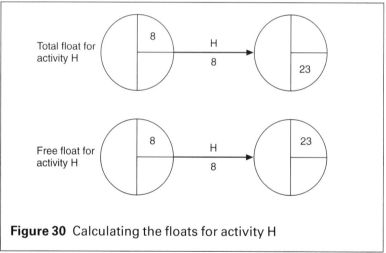

Figure 30 Calculating the floats for activity H

The programme evaluation and review technique

Governments find it particularly difficult to plan and control military projects. In the UK, plans to provide the army with an effective means of communication are currently running ten years late and are millions of pounds over budget. Such projects carry greater uncertainties because they are usually pushing at the edges of known technologies, and undertaken with a degree of secrecy.

The US Navy has developed a more sophisticated form of critical-path analysis, called the 'programme analysis and review technique', usually simply abbreviated to **PERT**. Its application is said to have resulted in the completion of the Polaris submarine nuclear missile programme two years ahead of schedule.

PERT involves the addition of *probability calculations* to network analysis. The duration of each activity is estimated on optimistic, most-likely and pessimistic bases, and these statistical estimates are then used to further evaluate the probability that a chosen critical path will actually turn out to be critical. It might be that a non-critical path containing potential float time is in fact more likely to be critical. This approach strengthens network analysis and enables more thorough analysis of possible paths.

KEY WORDS

Project environment	EST
Project definition	LFT
Critical-path analysis	Critical path
Objectives	Float time
Scope	Free float
Strategy	Total float
Scheduling	PERT
Nodes	

Further reading

Lock, D., *Project Management*, Gower, 1993.

Lockyer, K., and Gordon, J., *Critical Path Analysis and Other Project Network Techniques*, Pitman, 1991.

Miller, R. W., 'How to control and plan with PERT', *Harvard Business Review*, vol. 14, 1962.

Useful websites

Bized: www.bized.ac.uk/virtual/cb/factory/design/intro1.htm (the research and development part of project planning)

The Chartered Institute of Purchasing and Supply: www.cips.org (has good links to other sites)

Essay topic

Critically assess the contribution that critical-path analysis can make to the performance of a business organization. [25 marks]

Data response question

This task is based on an Edexcel sample paper issued in 2000. Imagine that a certain building project consists of a number of distinct activities, A to I, as shown in the diagram and table. Study the data and then answer the questions that follow.

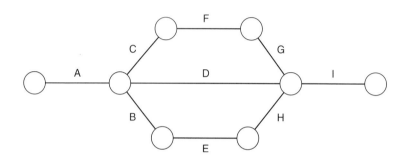

Activity	Duration in days	Labour requirements
A	1	4
B	3	6
C	5	4
D	2	3
E	3	6
F	4	6
G	4	5
H	2	4
I	2	9

1. (a) What is the earliest start date for each of activities C, H and I?
   [3 marks]
   (b) What is the latest finish time for each of the activities D, E and H? [3 marks]
2. Identify and calculate the duration of the critical path for this network. [3 marks]
3. (a) Explain what is meant by the term 'total float'. [2 marks]
   (b) Calculate the float times that exist on each activity. [3 marks]

Chapter Seven

Managing inventory

*The management of inventory is concerned with reconciling or
balancing two potentially conflicting objectives. The necessity of
holding stocks of raw materials, partly finished goods and completed
goods in order to meet fluctuations in demand from either the
production process or from final customers has to be balanced against
the costs of holding such stocks.*

Numerous references have already been made to the significance of
inventory or **stock control** in the efficient management of operations.
In this chapter consideration is given to particular techniques which
can be used to manage inventory.

The management of inventory is concerned with reconciling or
balancing two potentially conflicting objectives. The necessity of
holding stocks of raw materials, partly finished goods (**work in
progress**) and completed goods in order to meet fluctuations in demand
from either the production process or from final customers has to be
balanced against the costs of holding such stocks. All operations will
keep inventories of some kind, and they are usually classified as shown
in Figure 31.

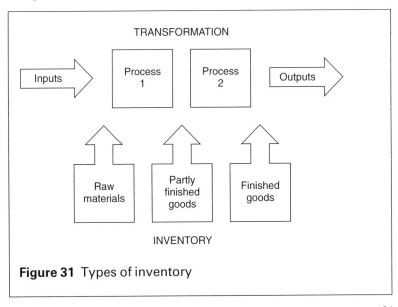

Figure 31 Types of inventory

- *Raw materials.* If the transformation process involves significant inputs of raw materials, a business may wish to insulate the production process from unanticipated fluctuations in supply. Moreover, cost savings might be possible when purchases of inputs are made in bulk.

- *Partly finished goods.* If the transformation process involves a number of different processes, each dependent upon the output of a previous stage, a business may choose to maintain buffer stocks at particularly significant points in the production process. This will allow longer production runs, provide an insurance against breakdowns in the production cycle and give greater flexibility in terms of the utilization of different machines for different tasks.

- *Finished goods.* Stocks may be kept of **finished goods**, especially if the demand is subject to seasonal variations, or to anticipate increases in future demand. The holding of stocks at this and the other stages of production is not always the result of a conscious decision. Stocks can build up at any stage as a result of mistakes and errors which can arise if marketing plans are not met or if inadequate stock-control procedures have been followed.

Inventory decisions

There are three key inventory decisions which organizations need to make: **volume, timing** and **control**.

Volume and timing decisions tend to be interrelated. Buying in larger volumes means longer gaps between deliveries. Conversely, smaller inputs will require more frequent deliveries.

Inventory control analysis

The volume of additions to inventory can be analysed graphically, as in Figure 32(a). Inventory levels are measured on the y (vertical) axis and time on the x axis. In this example, the order level is 800 units per month, giving an average inventory size of 400 units, as shown by the horizontal line. In the diagram it is assumed that stocks are used up at a constant rate, and that delivery times are both fixed and constant over time. When this be the case, a stable pattern of stock use and ordering will be maintained.

A similar chart can be used to illustrate an alternative ordering strategy that involves more frequent deliveries but results in carrying lower levels of inventory. Such a chart is shown in Figure 32(b). In this example, weekly orders of 200 units are delivered, giving an average inventory of 100.

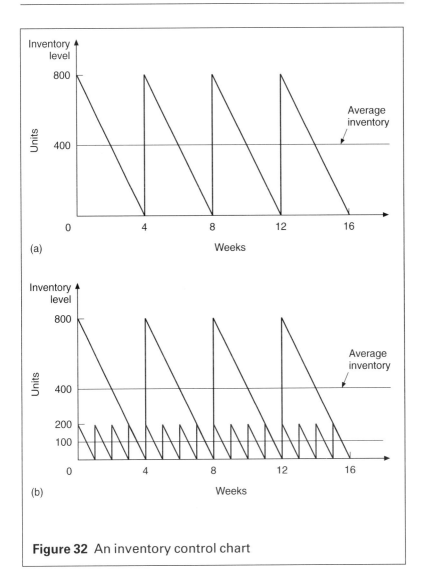

Figure 32 An inventory control chart

This diagrammatic treatment illustrates the different inventory levels and delivery schedules but does not indicate which would be most cost-effective. Additional data and analysis are required in order to choose between the alternative strategies. This is considered in the following section.

Inventory costs

Decisions about the volume and timing of additions to inventory have crucial cost implications. Some costs decrease as order size is increased. One reason for this is that time and resources have to be devoted to raising orders. In addition to these clerical costs, an organization may be faced with related costs in terms of changing over from producing one particular product to another. Hence, raising a small number of large orders will reduce ordering costs. Similarly, suppliers may offer discounts for larger orders, or charge higher prices for small deliveries.

Finally, running out of supplies, known as **stock-out**, is likely to involve costs in terms of lost sales and, worse, customer dissatisfaction. Stock-outs are more likely to occur when low levels of inventory are carried, so a business may be inclined to avoid this cost by carrying larger inventories. Together these costs are called **ordering costs**.

On the other hand, some inventory-related costs are likely to increase as order size is increased. Obviously, working capital will be tied up with stocks, especially as suppliers are likely to demand payment before revenue from related sales is received. High stock levels might therefore lead to larger overdrafts and higher interest payments, or will tie up capital which could be used more profitably elsewhere within the operation.

Storage costs – rent, warehousing, security, temperature control and the like – increase with the size of inventory. Also, carrying large stocks for long periods of time carries risks of spoilage and obsolescence (goods becoming out of date or out of fashion). The costs of carrying stock are called **holding costs**.

The relationship between these two sets oF inventory costs and the volume of orders is illustrated in Figure 33, where holding costs rise with the volume of an individual order while order costs decline. The cumulative effect of these conflicting cost pressures are illustrated in the total-cost curve. The point of intersection of the order costs and holding costs will represent the **economic order quantity**. In this case, this lies between the two alternatives previously illustrated.

Clearly any change in holding or ordering costs will result in the derivation of a new optimum. This is illustrated in Figure 34(a) for reduced holding costs (HC^2), and in Figure 34(b) for reduced ordering costs (OC^2).

Fluctuations in demand and inventory supply

The preceding analysis is based on steady and predictable levels of demand and supply of inventory. Few organizations operate in such a

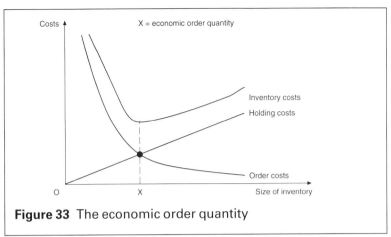

Figure 33 The economic order quantity

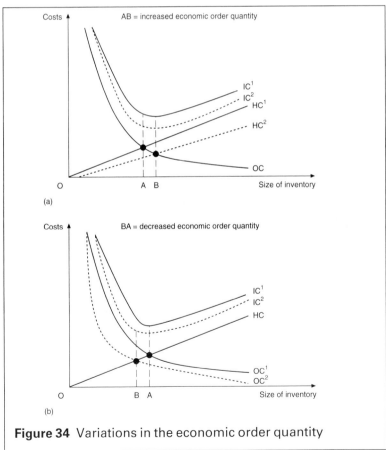

Figure 34 Variations in the economic order quantity

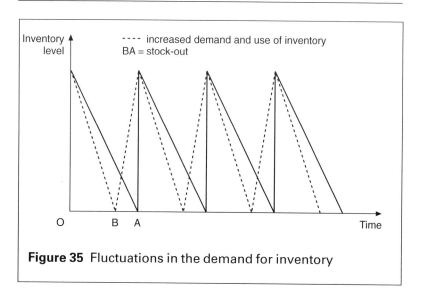

Figure 35 Fluctuations in the demand for inventory

stable and risk-free environment, but inventory control analysis can still be used to inform decisions.

For example, if there are increases in sales and consequent resource use, stocks will be depleted at a faster rate, indicated by a steepening of the gradient illustrated by the dotted line in Figure 35 (the solid line represents the inventory level shown in Figure 32(a)). If the timing of new orders is not changed to meet the increased demand for the final product, stock-out would occur, as shown by BA. To prevent this, a re-ordering point will have to occur earlier to allow new stocks to be delivered with no disruption to production.

The timing decision

The last section raised the issue of the timing of additional inventory, and in the earlier example it was assumed that deliveries were made instantaneously. Clearly, this is unrealistic – it is likely that there will be a lag between order and delivery.

This is illustrated in Figure 36, in which it is assumed that the lag between order and delivery will not exceed two weeks. This is known as the **lead-time**. Given the level of demand for inventory, stock-out would occur at the end of week 4. Given a lead-time of two weeks, re-ordering would be triggered when stocks fell to 400 units.

This analysis can be used further to help deal with fluctuations in both delivery times and demand for inventory. A business may decide

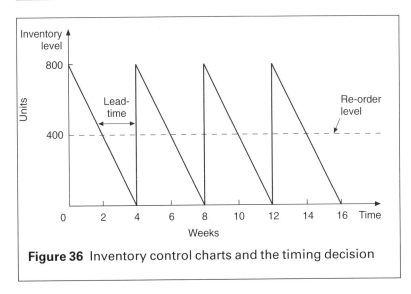

Figure 36 Inventory control charts and the timing decision

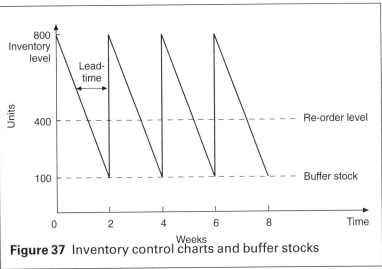

Figure 37 Inventory control charts and buffer stocks

to hold a **buffer stock** to cope with such variations. This is illustrated in Figure 37. The horizontal dotted line indicates the planned minimum stock level of 100 units. Re-ordering is triggered two weeks before this minimum stock level is reached. The risk associated with being faced with stock-out is reduced.

Inventory control

While the use of the foregoing graphical techniques helps to identify key decisions about the management of inventory, they represent a simplification of the situation faced by most organizations. A typical supermarket stocks 15 000 different product lines, and a modern photocopier consists of almost as many individual components. No matter what sophisticated market intelligence systems are used, consumer demand for most products on a given day or week is hard to predict with a high degree of accuracy – hence the complexity and challenge involved with the management and control of inventories.

One approach to making these tasks more manageable is to classify items by the value of their usage. Thus, those items making a significant contribution to sales, coupled with a high **usage rate,** would be more closely monitored and controlled than other items with a low usage rate and small contribution to sales. The justification of this approach is that if it were possible to carry lower stocks, or to prevent theft, of priority items there would be a more significant impact on profitability than would be the case with low-priority items.

Many organizations have devoted both time and resources to try to improve inventory control. Traditionally, stock-taking would be a key activity as improved inventory management has an immediate impact on profitability. Some businesses would actually close for **stock-taking.** All, or most staff, would be withdrawn from their normal duties and every partly finished and finished product would have been tracked down and recorded. These returns would be compared to documentary records of production and sales and any discrepancies would be noted.

Today, developments in ICT have revolutionized many aspects of stock control. Supermarkets such as Tesco have moved to fully automated systems which use **bar-coding** to record purchases at the point of sale, thus providing continually updated stock records, generating orders, communicating these to warehouses, scheduling deliveries and forecasting future demand. Although the use of ICT has speeded up these processes, it is still necessary to undertake manual checks. Thus, comparison of sales records and goods inwards should indicate the levels of stock held in stores and on shelves. These need to be checked to track levels of theft, and wastage. Hand held bar code readers are usually for this task.

```
                      KEY WORDS
Inventory                   Ordering costs
Stock control               Holding costs
Work in process             Economic order quantity
Finished goods              Lead-time
Volume                      Buffer stock
Timing                      Usage rate
Control                     Stock-taking
Stock-out                   Bar-coding
```

Further reading
Jewell, B., *An Integrated Approach to Business Studies*, Longman, 2000.

Montgomery, D., *Introduction to Statistical Quality Control*, John Wiley & Sons, 1991.

Oakland, J., and Fallowell, R., *Statistical Process Control: A Practical Guide*, Heinemann, 1990.

Wild, R., *Production and Operations Management*, Cassell, 1990.

Useful websites
Bized: www.bized.ac.uk/virtual/cb/factory/purchasing/intro1.htm (part of the virtual company devoted to inventory control)

International Purchasing and Supply Education & Research Association: www.ipsera.org/ (site of the professional body for those involved in chain management)

Essay topic
Discuss the contention that the contribution of just-in-time to business performance has been grossly exaggerated.

(a) Identify the aims of inventory control [4 marks]
(b) Explain the key inventory decisions. [6 marks]
(c) Discuss the contention that the contribution of just-in-time to business performance has been grossly exaggerated. [15 marks]

Data response question

This task is based on an AQA specimen paper issued in 2000. Study the piece below and the data given. Then answer the questions that follow.

Polar Ices has a small share of the West Country ice cream market. its biggest selling line is a range of ice lollies. These are very profitable, though the extreme seasonality of the sales causes many operational problems.

At present, the company copes with the summer peak by building up stocks earlier in the year. This is necessary because the factory only has the capacity to produce 140 000 units per month. Now the managing director is considering chaning to a Just in Time production system. He believes that enough will be saved from the cash tied up in stocks to pay for the new equipment and extra temporary workers.

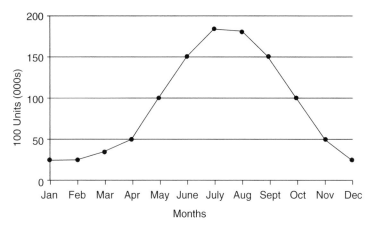

Figure A Polar Ices Ltd ice lolly sales, 1999

1. (a) Explain why Polar Ices needs to build up stocks in the early part of the year. [4 marks]
   (b) State and explain three likely effects of the company building up stocks. [6 marks]
2. (a) Explain the meaning of the term 'Just in Time production' (line 6) [3 marks]
   (b) Discuss whether Polar Ices should switch to Just in Time production. [8 marks]
3. The managing director has thought about batch production of chocolate in the winter months. Would you advise him to do this? Justify your answer. [9 marks]

Chapter Eight

Assuring quality

The development of quality systems is seen as a means of continually baring down paving the costs of production, while at the same time providing competitive advantage in those many markets in which competition is becoming increasingly intense.

Whether they be in the public or private sector, almost all organizations emphasize the importance of quality assurance, not just to operations management but also to the whole organization. The development of quality systems is seen as a means of continually baring down paving the costs of production, while at the same time providing competitive advantage in those many markets in which competition is becoming increasingly intense.

This chapter is devoted to:

- defining quality
- outlining traditional approaches to quality
- consideration of more modern approaches.

The significance of quality can by judged by what might be an apocryphal story about Oscar Klein. He was employed at the end of the production line of Model T Fords in the US, and his job was to check quality. Cars reaching the required standard carried his initials: hence the universal term **OK**.

Defining quality

While most organizations subscribe to the importance of quality, it is a hard characteristic to define. Quality can be seen in terms of simply the best – the best airline, computer or school. Quality can also be defined in terms of how closely a product or service matches its design specification or its '**fitness for purpose**', which focuses on how well a particular customer need is met.

The basic difference between these and other definitions of quality can be explained by reference to whose *perspective* is used – that of the producer or that of the consumer.

It is relatively easy for the producers of a product or service to define and measure quality by reference to how closely it meets its design specification, or some other objective measure of performance. The customer may, however, be indifferent to the technical specifications of a product or service. Customer judgements are often much more subjective, influenced by a host of related and unrelated factors. In particular, customer judgements will be affected by their expectations of the performance of a particular product or service, and by their actual experience in consuming the product or service.

The problem is that quality, like beauty, lies in the eye of the beholder. If enough customers perceive that the food and service in a particular restaurant is outstanding, then quality standards have been met irrespective of any more objective measures (subject, of course, to health and safety issues). This **subjective aspect of quality** is often exploited in marketing strategies by attempts to provide the customer with at least the illusion that they have had a 'quality' experience.

Customer judgements about quality are affected further as they are rarely undertaken without reference to price. Broadly speaking, the higher the price the higher the expectation that quality will be provided. Conversely, consumers might tolerate lower quality standards from those products or services that are perceived to be cheap.

As quality is difficult to define, it follows that setting up quality assurance systems is neither easy nor solely the responsibility of the operations manager. However, traditional approaches to quality assurance were firmly rooted within the production function.

Traditional approaches to quality

The image of Oscar Klein typifies traditional approaches to quality assurance, or 'quality control' as such functions were usually described. Oscar Klien's job was to check the Model T Fords as they rolled off the end of the production line. Every so often, he would see, hear or feel something that indicated that quality levels had not been met. That car would not receive Oscar Klein's 'OK' sticker.

The can in question would be withdrawn from the production line and dismantled for scrap and, to use a modern term, 'recycled'. While it is dangerous to make sweeping generalizations about traditional approaches to quality control, certain characteristics can be identified:

- 100 per cent quality is unobtainable
- quality control is a specialized function
- profits are more important than quality
- quality is best defined in terms of the extent to which products or services meet the design specifications.

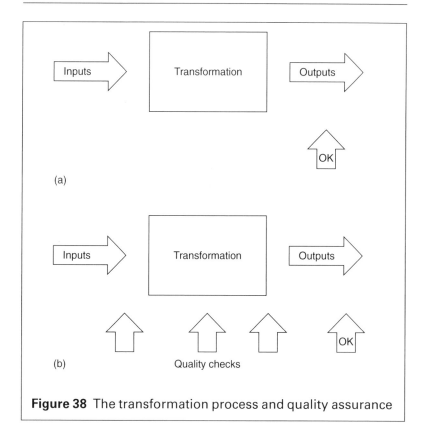

Figure 38 The transformation process and quality assurance

The application of these characteristics to the transformation process can take various forms. Most crudely, the Oscar Klein approach to quality assurance focuses on final outputs. This is shown in Figure 38(a).

In previous systems, the importance of craftsmanship and the use of a skilled workforce was considered sufficient to guarantee quality. While the introduction of quality control was a great advance on previous systems, this approach meant that errors and mistakes were identified only at the *end* of the production process (if they were identified at all).

The quality assurance process could be strengthened by the addition of extra quality control points which could lead to the earlier identification of and, even more importantly, the *avoidance* of substandard production. This is illustrated in Figure 38(b), in which inputs of resources are checked at different stages in production.

Statistical quality control

Employing Oscar Klein was a definite step forward in terms of raising the quality of Model T Fords, but it still left the inspection function up to the subjective assessment of a few individuals. The inspection processes outlined above have been further developed to provide a more thorough and objective sampling of outputs.

With the introduction of **statistical quality control**, random checks can be made and more sophisticated approaches developed. This can involve the application of a matrix similar to that used in Chapter 7 to assess optimum stock levels.

It may be possible to quantify the cost associated with failure to meet quality standards (the **defect cost**). This will include the cost associated with higher waste levels, the re-working of faulty outputs, dealing with complaints, more after-sales activity and lost sales. As illustrated in Figure 39, the defect cost will decline as the quality level rises.

On the other hand, taking steps to raise or maintain quality is also likely to have an associated cost (the **inspection cost**), including making more thorough inspections and undertaking preventative work to minimize substandard production. As illustrated in Figure 39, this cost rises as higher quality standards are sought.

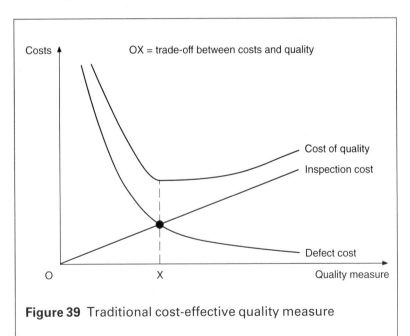

Figure 39 Traditional cost-effective quality measure

The defect and inspection costs can be added together, as shown on the diagram, to obtain the the **cost of quality**. The lowest point of this curve coincides with the intersection of the two individual cost curves, at a point that indicates the **cost-effective level of quality**.

In the example given, the organization might choose to aim for a **quality threshold** 95 per cent. Sampling techniques can then be used during the transformation process to see whether or not this 95 per cent quality threshold is being met.

Control charts

The data collected through statistical quality control can be further refined and used to identify possible causes of substandard output, when it is plotted against time on a **control chart**.

Thus to develop the example used earlier, actual quality measures can be recorded against time as shown in Figure 40(a). The 95 per cent quality threshold is represented by the horizontal line, and in this example quality standards appear to be improving over time. Nonetheless, quality levels show fluctuations around the trend, and this might be used to trigger closer investigation as to possible explanations of the variations. For instance, does the quality level fall during particular shifts, on certain days of the week or at certain times of the month?

Other statistical techniques can be used to control quality. The control chart can incorporate upper and lower control limits, as shown in Figure 40(b). Crossing of either of these can be interpreted as meaning that something significant has happened to the production process which needs to be investigated.

Criticisms of traditional approaches to quality

From the early 1960s, many UK businesses (along with their American and other western counterparts) developed a reputation for producing poor-quality goods. At the same time they were faced with increasingly strong competition from Japanese and other businesses based in the Far East.

Initially the success of these overseas competitors was dismissed with explanations like 'They use cheap labour and copy our inventions.' However, over a period of about 30 years the international success of the Japanese motorbike industry, followed by cars and trucks, electrical goods and computers, resulted in greater respect for these new competitors. Once this happened, many western businesses questioned their own practices more critically, and looked more closely at eastern business approaches in an attempt to find ways of improving **competitive performance**.

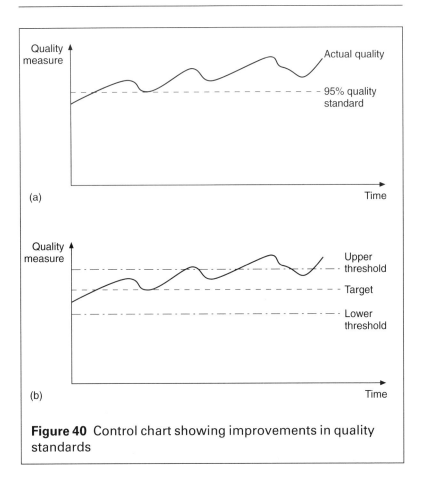

Figure 40 Control chart showing improvements in quality standards

Differences in approaches were typified by what has become another business legend, involving the giant American computer company IBM. The company subcontracted work on early computers to manufacturers in Japan, and specified that their suppliers must meet a 99 per cent quality threshold. The Japanese firms responded by ensuring that in every shipment of 100 computers, one would be faulty. They believed that they had an obligation to meet their customer's needs perfectly, and so they did!

The Japanese companies concerned were used to aiming for 100 per cent quality, illustrating fundamental differences in approach to operations management. These differences, and the responses of UK and American businesses, are considered more fully in the final section of this chapter.

Modern approaches to quality

Four related Japanese influences have had a significant effect on approaches to quality. They are:

- kaizen
- quality circles
- zero defects
- total quality management (TQM).

Kaizen

Kaizen means 'continuous improvement', and represents not just a different approach to quality but also a different philosophy to the improvement of operations management. It applies not just to the workplace but also to life.

According to this philosophy we should all strive to continually improve ourselves, our family, our social life and our work. Everyone should be involved in this process. From an operations management point of view, the net effect of all employees doing their best to improve is seen to be a more powerful agent of change than looking for significant and revolutionary changes (see Chapter 9 on lean production).

It follows from this that all employees should be involved in improving quality, rather than this being a specialized function given to particular workers. It also follows that, firstly, employees need to be empowered so that each can contribute to quality improvement, and, secondly, that team working and collaboration become more important to ensure that all contribute to the quality process. Such approaches to managing the human resource function do not come easily to some UK organizations, where rigid hierarchies, differences in status and entrenched attitudes are still common.

Quality circles

The introduction of quality circles is a strategy which has been copied from Japan by some organizations in order to encourage workers to contribute more fully to quality improvement. In the purest form of this concept, the membership of quality circles is voluntary, all members have equal status irrespective of their position within the organization and regular meetings take place to meet and discuss problems and develop potential solutions.

The philosophy behind this strategy to improve quality lies in the fact that employees often have, but do not necessarily use, an intimate technical understanding of the production process. Team-based approaches to problem-solving are often more powerful and effective than those which rely on individuals. The use of quality circles may also improve the motivation of workers.

However, as with the adoption of kaizen, this democratic approach to greater worker involvement in the quality process can produce tensions if it is not supported by the culture and working practices of the organization. Moreover, workers need to be relatively secure in their own future. For many employees, improvements involve change and change is often accompanied by insecurities associated with the fear of redundancy.

Zero defects
Setting the target of achieving zero defects is another significant shift away from traditional approaches to quality. If an organization determines that it will produce goods or provide services with no fault or problem, it will need to set in place quality assurance strategies at each and every stage in the transformation process. It follows that all workers must play their part, that design and capability must be constantly reviewed, and all links in the supply chain must be involved.

For example, significant purchasers of foodstuffs, such as the major supermarkets, can insist on quality systems and procedures being followed by the businesses in their supply chain. Similarly, some Japanese companies operating in the UK have a zero tolerance of supplier defects. This means that if any mistake is made in any aspect of the supply of a component, including an error on an invoice, or failure to deliver at a specified time, the delivery is refused and returned to the supplier.

Total quality management (TQM)
TQM refers to all the foregoing strategies and more. It developed out of the interaction between western and Japanese business theorists and Japanese industrialists, and places the customer at the beginning and end of the development of quality assurance systems. Total quality management:

- puts customers first
- involves the whole organization
- re-evaluates the costs of quality
- aims to get things right first time.

Putting the customer first
TQM systematically links quality improvements, from exploring how best to meet the needs and expectations of customers to all functional

aspects of an organization. In this way, all employees have a shared responsibility to improve on quality. For example, Xerox has developed an extremely thorough and comprehensive series of systems which use customer feedback to kick-start a whole process devoted to bringing about continuous improvement. This can involve all departments and divisions and incorporates quality circles, training entitlements for all workers and elements of kaizen. All these activities are designed to engineer out problems rather than make bad good.

Involving the whole organization

Another aspect of TQM that has been adopted with varying degrees of success by organizations is to take the concept of customer focus and apply that within the organization. As mentioned in Chapter 2, it is possible to envisage that the separate parts and sections of an organization are both producers and customers. This is used to help ensure that the whole organization focuses on quality. Each production unit strives to meet the demands of its customers, with the expectation that they will demand 100 per cent quality delivered at a price and time of their choosing – rather than having these crucial characteristics chosen by the producer.

Re-evaluating the cost of quality

Traditional approaches to costing quality, as illustrated in Figure 39, are built on a static model in which the cost associated with poor-quality output falls as expenditure on quality increases, whereas the cost of quality assurance rises. There is a clear trade-off between cost and quality, which leads to the point of cost-effectiveness at which a specified level of defect is deemed to be acceptable.

Advocates of TQM argue that this legitimizes failure and stops an organization from trying to improve continuously. Moreover, it can be argued that improvements to quality have implications in the long-run on customer satisfaction and the strengthening of demand, factors not recognized in the traditional model. Moreover, TQM can save resources if everyone shares a responsibility towards improving quality, because the costs of separate inspection and control are reduced. Hence there is a dynamic relationship between quality improvement and, ultimately, increased profitability.

Getting it right first time

TQM further strengthens the quality function by being *proactive* rather than *reactive*. Traditional quality systems are built around reacting to errors and mistakes and ensuring that they do not reach the customer.

Such a process can be wasteful and does not stimulate processes to actually prevent mistakes. TQM encourages organizations to look at all operations – especially design – in an attempt to ensure that production is 'right first time'. This is a logical development of the kaizen principle and zero defects.

KEY WORDS

OK	Quality threshold
Fitness for purpose	Control chart
Subjective aspect of quality	Competitive performance
Statistical quality control	Kaizen
Defect cost	Quality circles
Inspection cost	Zero defects
Cost of quality	Total quality management
Cost-effective level of quality	

Further reading

Bank, J., *The Essence of Total Quality Management*, Prentice Hall, 1992.

Drummond, H., *The Quality Movement*, Kogan Page, 1992.

Oakland, J., *Total Quality Management*, Butterworth–Heinemann, 1992.

Peters, T., and Austin, N., *A Passion for Excellence*, HarperCollins, 1982.

Essay topic

Choose a local business organization and assess the effectiveness of its quality assurance systems. [25 marks]

Useful websites

Institute of Quality Assurance: www.iqa.org/ (a British professional association)

Industry Week: www.industryweek.com (a US site which includes articles on current quality issues)

Industrial Society: www.indsoc.com (site of the society for authorized users only)

Data response question

This task is based on an AQA specimen paper issued in 2000. Read the piece below before answering the questions.

Peak practice

Ten years ago, Sobhan and Mike quit the cleaning business and bought the *Peak Heights* pub in the Peak District. The price of £240 000 was financed by the sale of their home in Sutton Coldfield and a £150 000 mortgage from a finance house. Soon after they bought the pub, the interest rate reached as high as 18 per cent, which caused them huge financial difficulties. Today's rate of 8 per cent is far more manageable.

When they bought it, the pub was mainly aimed at local trade. It was a long-standing destination for people from local villages or from as far away as Chesterfield. Its sales turnover was about £2000 per week. Siobhan and Mike noticed that the public bar was under-used and decided to rename it the Travellers' Bar. They steadily built up a tourist trade by advertising in Tourist Board publications and by offering what travellers wanted – good food, a wide range of beers and plenty of advice on local walks and tourist sites.

In 1995 turnover stabilized at £3600 a week. Aware that competition was increasing locally, the couple decided to start an in-house micro-brewery. This cost £6000 to set up, but more importantly it took Mike two days a week to produce the 45 gallons of local, real ale. It hardly seemed worth the effort, but Mike believed it was an important point of differentiation. Locals and tourists both liked sampling Mike's *Peaking Early* and *Peak Condition* ales. In 1997 *The Good Pub Guide* made *Peak Heights* 'Best Pub in Derbyshire', which helped build trade still further.

By 1998 the weekly turnover had risen to £4500 and their thoughts turned to a new proposition. Often they were asked for a room for the night. Did they do bed and breakfast? They even had phone calls from America. Although they knew that trade would be very seasonal, they decided to look further into this business opportunity. To convert the pub's first floor into six bedrooms with en-suite facilities would cost £120 000. Assuming a 50 per cent occupancy rate, Siobhan estimated that turnover would be boosted by one-third. This additional trade would have a profit margin of 60 per cent.

Another factor to consider was the effect on the three full-time staff. Instead of living in, they would have to live elsewhere. All three had made it clear that they would have to find new jobs. This would be a great shame as the friendly atmosphere in the bars, restaurant and kitchen was important to customers. It also helped the profit margins because wastage levels were exceptionally low. The staff knew how much to order and how to minimize waste in the bars and especially the restaurant. Quite simply, they cared. This helped Mike and Siobhan enjoy their work, but also saved them from having to set up detailed systems for quality or stock control.

Mike felt sure that they should expand. It would build a stronger business to hand over to their twenty-year-old son who was currently at catering college. Siobhan was not so sure. They were agreed, though, that they must make a decision soon.

1. To help manage the operational side of the business, Siobhan and Mike intend to upgrade the ICT provision. They want a better system for stock ordering and management. Assess the possible effects of a move to computerize operations management at *Peak Heights*. [12 marks]
2. How might the business be helped by using critical-path analysis to plan the bedroom conversions? [8 marks]

Chapter Nine

Raising quality

There is little doubt that the quality revolution has created lucrative financial opportunities for a small army of consultants, but the lasting impact on quality and the competitiveness of UK industry is more debatable.

Chapter 8 contained a contrast between those approaches to quality which can be described as 'traditional' and those associated with Japanese and other influences typified by total quality management (**TQM**). Efforts to improve the quality of operations management in the UK and other western countries from the 1970s onwards have spawned a range of initiatives, some driven by **business gurus**. There is little doubt that the quality revolution has created lucrative financial opportunities for a small army of consultants, but the lasting impact on quality and the competitiveness of UK industry is more debatable.

This chapter describes various attempts to improve quality and considers some of the issues which impact on the success or otherwise of these operations management changes. The following 'initiatives' are considered:

- quality standards
- benchmarking
- re-engineering
- lean production.

Quality standards

Many of us are familiar with the various **kitemarks** which companies use to indicate to potential customers and others that particular standards have been met. Both governments and independent bodies are responsible for establishing standards and ensuring that individual companies meet them.

For example, the European Union lays down minimum standards for all electrical goods, which are legally required to carry the *communanté européan* (CE) symbol. Many companies use the Investor in People logo to indicate that they have conformed to standards relating to effective human resource management.

Increasingly, UK firms are adopting the standards laid down by the British Standards Institute in **BS 5750** and by its international equivalent, the International Standards Organization, in **ISO 9000** standards. These relate directly to quality. This kitemark is earned when companies document all business processes, produce a quality manual and develop quality management systems. While it is debatable as to how much significance consumers attach to products or services carrying the BS or ISO kitemark, the standards are used by large and dominant industrial and commercial customers to lever quality standards operated by organizations in their supply chain upwards.

Most kitemarking initiatives are essentially about documenting systems. This may sound unnecessarily bureaucratic, but for many organizations the process of documentation can be more important than the outcomes. This applies particularly to older established organizations whose employees follow procedures because that is the way things have always been done. Forcing organizations to establish and record quality systems can create positive changes and improvements, especially when employees are encouraged to participate fully in the process.

The profit motive in the private sector forces competitive firms to think and act on quality issues. These incentives are not always so apparent to less competitive organizations. Thus, the use of kitemarking can be particularly important in raising awareness about quality issues in public-sector and not-for-profit businesses. Many schools and colleges sport a variety of logos on their publicity literature, including Investor in People, 'charter marks' and various claims to support equal opportunities.

It can be argued that kitemark collection stimulates quality improvements. Government policies about inspection of schools, colleges, hospitals and other public services, and the insistence on what are called '**best value** reviews', also force local councils to consider the impact of their services on 'customers' more critically than would otherwise be the case.

While it can be argued that ISO 9000 and related systems involve considerable time and expense in documenting systems and procedures, there are clear benefits from the vigorous appraisal of practices which may have developed in an *ad hoc* and unsystematic way. A more fundamental criticism of these approaches is that they do not incorporate modern approaches to statistical quality control, nor do they encourage the constant improvements associated with continuous improvement.

Benchmarking

One of the first companies to use benchmarking to improve performance and quality standards was Xerox. It is an excellent example of a US-owned multinational company that was suddenly almost overwhelmed by Japanese competition.

Xerox had jealously protected its competitive advantage in the production of photocopiers by the judicious use of literally hundreds of patents over many of the components contained within photocopiers. That monopoly position was challenged by the UK's Monopolies Commission (now called the Competition Commission), and the company was suddenly faced with foreign competition. Xerox rapidly lost market share to companies like Canon, and there followed a serious re-evaluation of all aspects of operations management. This involved comparing the features, assembly and components of its products with those who were identified as being the best competitors. Xerox discovered that it:

- used many more suppliers of components
- rejected ten times more machines on its production line than did its best competitor
- took twice as long to get its products to customers.

Although Xerox still faces strong competition, this benchmarking resulted in significant improvements in quality, a commitment to TQM, and a focus on improving **relationships in the supply chain**.

The relative success of Xerox led other companies to benchmark, and such practices are now directly supported and encouraged by the Department of Trade and Industry (DTI) in an attempt to promote international competitiveness. The DTI has supported comparisons between UK companies and foreign competitors in an attempt to improve all aspects of business performance, especially operations management.

The UK government has identified particular industrial-sector industries as being crucial to the future economic success of the country. These include the print and packaging industry, chemicals and food processing. Government-funded benchmarking has involved comparing the performance of UK businesses with international competitors against a range of criteria.

Some of these studies make sombre reading from a UK perspective. Quality levels in many firms lag behind international competitors, and are especially affected by lower skill levels, lower levels of investment in both training and new technology, poor management and poor long-term planning. Ironically, these were the kind of deficiencies identified in the 1970s to explain lost export markets and higher levels of foreign imports!

The successful use of benchmarking involves agreement as to what aspects an organization's or industry's performance can be measured, the collection of data and the analysis of results. Even quite simple data comparisons on price, delivery times and defects can provide the basis for useful analysis of the strengths and weaknesses of particular organizations and industries. However, care has to be taken that comparisons be made on like-for-like data, and that the use of simple statistical measures does not mask or ignore more complex social and cultural differences.

Benchmarking can require a high level of inter-company collaboration, but it does not have to involve comparisons between businesses in the same industry or sector, especially when issues of competitive advantage may make businesses reluctant to share data they regard as commercially sensitive. Some businesses have gained much by benchmarking particular functions across different industries and sectors.

For example, Westland Helicopters improved its inventory management systems by collaborating with the supermarket chain Safeway, for whom effective inventory control was one of the main factors affecting its business performance. Similarly, Rover cut its testing times in half following benchmarking against Honda. Lucas simplified its staff grading system as a result of comparisons with German electrical manufacturers.

Another company whose experience of benchmarking was a little more complex is Tesco. Its autocratic former owner, Jack Cohen, was said to respect Marks & Spencer, especially in regard to its management and motivation of workers as a model on which to improve the quality of service experienced by customers. It is said that he copied many of Marks & Spencer's innovations – subsidized canteens, hair care and chiropody for the staff – and was perplexed that this positive treatment for staff was not mirrored by improved levels of customer care. Tesco had a reputation for staff who were rude and indifferent to customers' needs. Eventually a study was undertaken which showed that the main factor leading to poor customer service was the poor interpersonal skills of many middle managers. It is said that they treated staff badly, and the staff responded with poor levels of motivation and indifference to customers' needs. Tesco responded by investing in a programme of personal skills development for middle managers. Those who could not adapt to the new, more caring and considerate attitude to staff were forced to find alternative employment.

Re-engineering

Re-engineering is a particular combination of eastern and western business practice, which has it origins in the concerns about loss of international competitiveness considered earlier.

Re-engineering is about both quality and company organization. As a business strategy, re-engineering developed in the US in the early 1990s and, as with other initiatives to improve business performance, generated profitable business for consultants and trainers.

Its proponents argue that traditional hierarchical organizational structures encourage workers to look and defer to those further up the hierarchy. Everything points upwards to the top, making the managing director and senior executives the focus of corporate culture and behaviour. It is argued that organizations need to be re-engineered in order to focus on the most important factor in determining business performance – the customer; and usually those workers at the bottom of a traditional hierarchy are closest to customers. Employees should look outwards rather than upwards and within.

This particular approach can be seen as a different way of presenting or even marketing those concepts associated with TQM, but the conscious use of the term 're-engineering' places greater importance on achieving quality outcomes by re-organizing existing organizational structures.

Typically this would involve the removal of a layer or layers of 'middle managers'. Employees lower down the hierarchy would be empowered to take greater responsibilities. Those at the top would be brought closer to customers; costs would be reduced while at the same time organizational focus on meeting customers' needs would be strengthened.

Job losses could be one outcome which would be more difficult to manage. Workers are unlikely to want to be involved in processes which could ultimately result in the loss of their employment! This may point to a fundamental difference between re-engineering and TQM. The latter focuses on continual and gradual improvements, whereas re-engineering sees quality improvements arising from more radical structural and organizational changes.

Such radical and revolutionary approaches can have unfortunate outcomes, as typified by the privatization of British Rail. Many of the private-sector companies which took over sections of the formerly publicly owned monopoly reasoned that they would be able to increase profitability and returns by applying modern private-sector business approaches. These included a much greater focus on profitability as an objective rather than some notion of public service. One of the immediate outcomes was to devise operations management systems which theoretically would make better use of available capacity (trains) and more effective use of skilled workers (train drivers). This re-engineering involved reducing the number of employees. Many of the most skilled workers took advantage of early redundancy packages, leaving the newly privatized companies short of much-need skills. Companies such as Great Western and Connex coped with shortages by cutting services and creating an image of declining quality. Re-engineering in this context reduced rather than improved business performance.

Lean production

Lean production is another operations management strategy developed from comparative research into US and Japanese approaches to operations management. When Toyota was planning for expansion after World War II, it concluded that American mass production techniques produced excessive amounts of **muda** – wasted time, work and materials. As a result Toyota determined to remove as much waste as possible from its operations management. The company adopted policies of continuous improvement which included:

- investing in multi-purpose machine tools that could be quickly re-tooled to meet changed and different functions
- investing in training to multi-skill the workers
- adopting just-in-time approaches to inventory management (see Chapter 7)
- emphasizing the importance of quality.

These changes were considered to be the responsibility of both workers and managers, and their successful implementation gave Toyota considerable cost advantages over competitors. Thus in the 1980s Japanese car manufacturers could ship their products half way round the world to European markets and still undercut European manufacturers on price. Similarly, it was shown in 1990 that General Motors in the US took 40.7 person-hours to produce a car, whereas Toyota used 18.

Lean production is also associated with three business buzzwords or concepts of the 1990s: **labour flexibility**, **outsourcing** and **core activities**.

- *Flexibility of labour.* One way of increasing the ease of varying inputs of labour into the transformation process is to employ agency or contract workers, who are technically employed by companies such as Manpower. The organization actually using these workers is freed from various legal obligations in terms of employment rights, and can effectively hire and fire at will.

- *Outsourcing.* This is another form of subcontracting. Particular parts of the transformation process are subcontracted to specialist companies. This is now common in terms of the distribution of products, but can be applied to any business function.

These two business practices can allow companies to concentrate on their *core activity* or business. Thus, British Airway's core business is making profits out of flying people to where they want to go. BA subcontracts catering, maintenance and other functions to specialist firms.

One problem with lean production, re-engineering, and related strategies to raise quality and improve business performance is that a greater focus on designing operations management functions to directly meeting customer requirements with a minimum of waste can result in lower demands for labour, at both production and management levels. Thus, in the recession in the early 1990s, both terms became synonymous with redundancy and growing unemployment. As noted earlier, workers are far less likely to contribute fully to raising quality and cutting costs if they are in fear of losing their jobs as a result. Conversely, when an economy is expanding rapidly (as in the UK in the late 1990s), workers find it easier to find alternative employment and are reluctant to work for agencies. Alternatively the cost of employing agency workers rises, limiting the advantages of greater labour flexibility.

Raising quality: the UK experience

There is little doubt that there has been a quality revolution for many UK organizations over the last decade. Tesco suffered for years from a down-market image but now has the largest market share in food retailing. Nissan now records higher levels of productivity per worker in its UK plants than in those in Japan. Although still troubled, Rover now produces cars with far fewer defects than eight years ago. Even schools, hospitals and local government recognize that there are benefits in striving to meet customers' demands rather than ignoring them.

However, as indicated in the section on benchmarking, many UK firms still fall short of their international competitors. There are a number of competing explanations as to why quality standards for many UK organizations could be further improved. These include:

- flawed translation of **the Japanese model**
- **short-termism**
- **under-investment in capital and training.**

Flawed translation of the Japanese model

It should be clear from this and the previous chapter that Japanese approaches to quality have been successful because some aspects of Japanese culture and social practice complement them. In Japan, it is always considered polite and appropriate behaviour to meet the needs of your customer, to seek enlightenment and maintain a harmonious relationship with other people by taking small steps to improve and to accept social demands and expectations far more passively than might be the case in the West.

Also, until recently most Japanese organizations considered that they had more extensive obligations to their workers than would be the case in the UK. Job security, healthcare and social events formed part of these binding sets of obligations. Modern Japanese business practice, as it developed in the latter half of the twentieth century, fitted cultural traditions and expectations.

In the UK, however, such a complex and all-embracing sense of mutual obligation between employer and worker has not been common.

UK industrial relations, particularly in the 1960s and 70s, were characterized by mistrust and conflict. The recessions of the early 1980s and 90s resulted in high levels of unemployment. Some UK employers place great importance on having a flexible workforce, enabling them to hire and fire at short notice. On the other hand, Japanese culture and traditions encourage team-working, collaboration and loyalty to employers. It can be argued that the UK's culture and traditions have the opposite effect. Team-working, worker empowerment and greater equality in the workplace are seen as unrealistic and inappropriate.

Another indication of less harmonious industrial relations in the UK has been the antagonism and conflict that, until recently, characterized the relationship between many employers and trade unions. Confrontational attitudes are hardly conducive to team-working and shared notions of working towards a common good. However, there is some evidence from the late 1990s that employers and trade unions see common advantage in collaboration.

Companies such as Tesco, Ford and BA Systems have attempted to involve trade unions much more extensively in programmes designed to improve quality. There are signs that this changed relationship can provide a very powerful strategy to involve workers in raising quality and improvements in both training and education.

Short-termism

Japanese companies have been prepared to plan and invest for the long term. It is argued that these Japanese companies have viewed the development of world market dominance as an important business objective, and this required long-term investment both in plant and training. The influence of this has not been confined to Japan, as the UK had benefited greatly from Japanese investment. Such long-term planning has until recently contributed to greater job security and loyalty to employers.

Many commentators on UK industry have pointed to the adverse effect of short-termism (a term used to describe a focus on short-term profits and rewards). This is sometimes blamed on the heavy reliance by large companies on the stock market as a source of capital. Responding to fluctuations in share prices can lead companies to make major decisions about investment, product development, training budgets and the like which may not contribute to longer-term growth and development.

It can be argued that the pursuit of short-term objectives is not conducive to the creation of conditions in which total approaches to quality are likely to be successful. Thus, the adoption of lean production or re-engineering, and even TQM, might be seen as a means of cutting short-term costs, boosting profits, and raising share prices rather than a longer-term attempt to improve business performance by focusing on quality improvements.

Under-investment in capital and training

Many industrial and economic studies have highlighted what might be another dimension to short-termism – persistent relative under-investment in both capital and training. UK workers have poorer educational qualifications than most of our European competitors, and some are also lower than in Singapore and South Korea.

Similarly, levels of investment in new plant and machinery compare unfavourably with the UK's competitors. It can be argued that improving quality will occur only if it is accompanied by improved levels of training and higher levels of investment.

KEY WORDS

TQM
Business gurus
Quality standards
Benchmarking
Re-engineering
Lean production
Kitemarks
BS 5750
ISO 9000
Best value

Relationships in the supply
  chain
Muda
Labour flexibility
Outsourcing
Core activities
The Japanese model
Short-termism
Under-investment in capital and
  training

Further reading

Adams, S., *The Dilbert Principle*, Boxtree Press, 1997.
Drucker, P., *The New Realities*, Butterworth–Heinemann, 1989.
Handy, C., *The Age of Unreason*, Century Business, 1989.
Hutton, W., *The State We're In*, Cape, 1995.
Peters, T., *The Tom Peters Seminar*, Macmillan, 1994.

Useful websites

Confederation of British Industry: www.fitforthefuture.co.uk (CBI site
  devoted to raising quality)
Trades Union Congress: www.tuc.org.uk (access to trade union
  perspectives on modern approaches to quality)
m4i: www.m4i.org.uk (site devoted to raising quality)

Essay topics

1. Assess the contribution made to improving quality in the UK by the
  adoption of Japanese business practices. [25 marks]
2. Compare and contrast Conservative and Labour Party policies to
  improve the competitiveness of UK businesses. [25 marks]

Data response question

This task is based on an Edexcel Marketing and Production specimen
paper issued in 2000. Study the piece below and the other data given,
and then answer the questions that follow.

Harry Ramsden's plc

Harry Ramsden's plc is no mere fish and chip shop. There are 36 restaurants where fresh fish is served in an atmosphere created with glass chandeliers and by smartly dressed staff. The chain has created a distinct theme. More outlets have been franchized for overseas operations as far afield as Australia, Hong Kong and Saudi Arabia. Harry Ramsden's has become an international brand name.

However, losses of £1.9 million in 1998–99 have forced management to rethink the marketing strategy. The firm, established over 50 years ago, is now operating in an industry where themed restaurants such as Planet Hollywood and Hard Rock Café are common and the competition is getting fiercer. Despite the growth in the market (see Table A), Harry Ramsden's has failed to maintain its market share. Chairman John Barnes has been quoted as believing the future is in the opening of small-scale restaurants rather than the large 200-seater establishments favoured in the past.

Table A The market for eating out (£ billions)

	UK expenditure on eating out	Fast-food sales
1997	22.6	6.0
1998	23.6	6.4
2004 forecast	31.0	8.4

Producing the right meal at the right time in the right place is a critical factor in achieving success in fast-food chains. With the rising costs of raw materials, their short shelf-life and the pattern of daily and weekly sales, batch production is the preferred method. The development of a large number of small-scale units to be supplied by the logistics section of Harry Ramsden's will mean a sophisticated stock-control system, particularly as costs per meal are likely to rise.

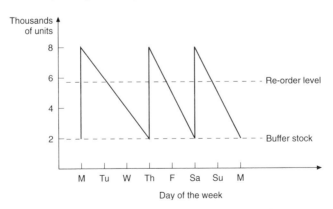

Figure A Model stock control graph for small unit restaurant

1. Using the stock control graph shown, state:
   (a) the re-order quantity [2 marks]
   (b) the weekly usage quantity [2 marks]
   (c) the number of orders each week. [2 marks]
2. Evaluate the factors which would influence Harry Ramsden's when deciding upon the buffer stock level and the re-order quantity.

   [20 marks]
3. Evaluate the case for and against adopting a just-in-time approach to stock-holding in the fast-food industry. [20 marks]

Conclusion

This book has been written to introduce students of business to operations management. This is a key business function and one that is often overlooked in comparison with, say, marketing or financial management. Nonetheless, efficient and effective operations management is the cornerstone of any successful business organization. The concepts used in this book should help students to appreciate how the modelling of operations management in different ways can be used to highlight key decisions and improve business performance.

The first chapter provides and outline of input–output approaches to the modelling of the transformation process that is at the heart of operations management. The contribution of buffering to smoothing out production was considered, as are those factors that might be useful in explaining why operations management may differ between organizations.

These themes were developed in Chapter 2, in which it is argued that the choice of production method is likely to be closely related to the volume and variety of outputs that are produced. Low-volume high-variety outputs are associated with project or one-off production, while high-volume low-variety outputs usually involve continuous production methods. Eastern business approaches – including 'just-in-time', 'continuous improvement' and 'zero defects' – have had a significant impact on traditional approaches to operations management.

Chapter 3 was devoted to various aspects of costs, including the identification of variable and fixed costs. This underpins the development of break-even analysis to establish the lowest level of sales necessary to avoid making a loss. Various methods used to account for indirect costs are considered, and finally economies and diseconomies of scale were explained. The former helps us understand why some industries were dominated by a few businesses, while in others inefficiencies associated with size can lead to demergers and the breaking up of large organizations.

Location is the operations management issue that was considered in Chapter 4. Location decisions can sometimes be understood by examination of the relative force of those factors pulling operations closer to markets, or closer to the source of raw materials. Many locations can, however, be explained only in terms of a combination of historical accident and inertia. Modern developments, especially in transport, electronic communications and technology transfer, have resulted in the development of both global markets and much more footloose organizations.

Chapter 5 focused on planning and controlling decisions faced by all organizations. The particular nature of the transformation process can have a direct effect on planning and control mechanisms, which are also affected by the nature of the demand for the product or service. It is far easier to plan to meet a stable and predictable demand than one that fluctuates unpredictably. Planning and control mechanisms can have a major effect on other functional aspects of an organization, especially in terms of stock levels, cash flow and responsiveness to customers. The final section of this chapter looked at wider strategic considerations, whereby the capacity of an organization can best be matched to fluctuations in demand. One of the most significant current developments in business is the search to develop quicker and more flexible responses to demand.

Project management techniques were examined in Chapter 6, and considerable attention is given to 'critical-path analysis' (CPA). This is a powerful tool that is used to both plan and control projects. CPA has been developed into an even more powerful tool (PERT) by the addition of probability calculations for each activity. Both techniques need to be used within a systematic framework of project management. This should include a critical assessment of the environment in which projects take place, clearly defined objectives and thorough planning.

Chapter 7 delved into the management of inventory. Inventory levels have to be controlled to reconcile fluctuations in both the demand and supply of stocks. An organization that fails to manage inventory properly is likely to be faced with stock-outs, redundant stocks, cash flow difficulties and poor profitability. Conversely, a well-managed inventory will contribute to improved business performance. These processes have been revolutionized by the application of information communications technology (ICT) and the use of bar-code technologies.

Modern and traditional approaches to quality were considered in Chapter 8. Both approaches acknowledge the importance of quality, and both have resulted in techniques of quality assurance such as statistical process control that are widely used. Modern approaches emphasize the importance of quality throughout organizations, whereas more traditional approaches may tolerate certain levels of defect.

Chapter 9 was also about quality, and introduce students into the important debate within business about how best to raise quality standards. The successes of Japanese and other eastern corporations in the 1970s and 80s forced many UK and western businesses to develop strategies to promote a greater focus on continual quality improvements. There is considerable evidence that many UK businesses in both the private and public sectors have significantly raised the quality of their outputs. However, it is argued that some of the enthusiasm to emulate Japanese business practice may have been misplaced, especially in those organizations pursuing short-term objectives, investing little in training and capital, and characterized by confrontational labour relations.

Index